MINDVAULTS

MINDVAULTS

Sociocultural Grounds for Pretending and Imagining

Radu J. Bogdan

The MIT Press
Cambridge, Massachusetts
London, England

MIT Press books may be purchased at special quantity discounts for business or sales promotional use. For information, please email special_sales@mitpress.mit.edu or write to Special Sales Department, The MIT Press, 55 Hayward Street, Cambridge, MA 02142.

This book was set in Stone Serif and Stone Sans by Toppan Best-set Premedia Limited. Printed and bound in the United States of America.

Library of Congress Cataloging-in-Publication Data

Bogdan, Radu J.
Mindvaults : sociocultural grounds for pretending and imagining / Radu J. Bogdan.
  p. cm.
Includes bibliographical references and index.
ISBN 978-0-262-01911-8 (hardcover : alk. paper)
1. Imagination. 2. Imagination in children. 3. Social psychology. 4. Social perception 5. Social cognitive theory. 1. Title.
BF408.B565 2013
153.3—dc23
                        2012036428

10 9 8 7 6 5 4 3 2 1

To my beloved Catalina,
for whom life is a constant exercise in imagination

Imagination is a new psychological process for the child; it is not present in the consciousness of the very young child, is totally absent in animals, and represents a specifically human form of conscious activity.

—Lev Vygotsky, *Mind in Society*

Contents

Preface   xiii
Introduction   xvii

I QUESTIONS   1

1 What Sort of Evolution?   5

1.1 Intuitive Debut   6
1.2 An Assortment of Puzzles   9
1.3 Possible Explanations   13
1.4 Evolutionary Turn to Ontogeny   16

2 What Sort of Ontogeny?   29

2.1 The Ape Connection   30
2.2 Sociocultural Activism   34
2.3 Unique Ontogeny for Unique Thoughts   38
2.4 Intuitive Psychology: The Driving Force   42

3 What Sort of Competence?   47

3.1 Identity Crises   49
3.2 The Competence Angle   56
3.3 Metamental Rehearsals   62
3.4 The Structure of the Argument   70

II DEVELOPMENTAL ANSWERS   73

Before Four: Playing with Culture   75

4 Early Foundations   77

4.1 Projection   78
4.2 Play   83
4.3 Naive Psychology   87
4.4 Imitation   90
4.5 Executive Readiness   92

5 Pretending   97

5.1 Cultural Challenges   99
5.2 Views about Pretending   107
5.3 The Action Angle   113
5.4 Role Impersonation in Sociocultural Action   117
5.5 Limitations   123
5.6 Contributions   127

After Four: Others and Self   137

6 Change of Mind   139

6.1 Increasingly Offline   142
6.2 A New Executive   145
6.3 Metarepresenting Others   149
6.4 Their Own Minds   158

7 Imagining   163

7.1 New Challenges: Juvenile Sociopolitics   164
7.2 Transition? Imaginary Companionship   167
7.3 Clues from Autobiographical Memory   170
7.4 Strategizing   175
7.5 Competence Transfer   187

8 Epilogue 195

8.1 Summation 195
8.2 Speculation 197
8.3 Why Evolution Matters 198

Appendix: Intuitive Psychology as Mind Designer 203

A.1 A Basic and Natural Connection 204
A.2 The Developmental Connection 208
A.3 Implications for Mindvaulting 215

Glossary 217
References 221
Index 233

Preface

Unpacking the metaphoric title and somewhat cryptic subtitle of this book may be the simplest, most direct way of introducing its content. According to the dictionary, *to vault* is to jump or leap over an obstacle or out of an enclosure, with the aid of a support or prop such as hands or a pole. The human mind—and apparently it alone—is able consciously and deliberately to vault itself cognitively out of the enclosure of current perception, motivation, emotion, and action, and leap over to future, past, possible, or even impossible facts, situations, or scenarios. Perhaps the most generic—but amorphous—expression of what I call *mindvaulting* is thinking. Somewhat narrower in scope and somewhat better studied, pretending and imagining are the first documented forms of mindvaulting that develop in human childhood. They will be the focus of this inquiry, with imagination in the forefront.

The dictionary also tells us that a *vault* is a network of arches configuring a roof over the interior of a building. Think of the mind as such a building, and the vault as a network of high-level (rooftop) mental abilities employed in reasoning, deliberate planning, thoughtful communication, reflective decision making, art creation, technological innovation, and scientific theorizing. These abilities can be subsumed collectively under the old-fashioned but still useful notion of *intellect*—the arched roof of the human mind, so to speak.

It turns out that compared to the crania of various Homo precursors, those of modern humans are actually higher. Luckily for my metaphor, paleoanthropologists call this development *vaulting* and suspect a connection with modern cognitive evolution. Could this actually be a connection with the modern intellect? I think so, and will argue that pretending and imagining can be viewed as crucial steps on the ontogenetic staircase to the intellect, and that imagining in particular can be viewed as the engine of the intellect.

Given this reading and the significance of mindvaulting, the questions I want to ask—the central questions of this book—are, Why mindvaulting? and With what resources? And more specifically, Why pretending and imagining? And again, With what resources? It turns out, in my view, that ontogeny is a genuine, active, and fertile territory of evolution; only modern human ontogeny evolved capacities for pretending and imagining, and hence for an intellect; and therefore, only an evolutionary look at ontogeny as *developmental evolution* can answer the questions just asked.

My inquiry reveals that unprecedented in other animal minds, first pretending and later imagining develop for *reasons* that are unique and specific to human childhood, out of a variety of *roots* or sources—some biologically deep and old, and others historically recent. In particular, my inquiry finds the most potent reasons for pretending and imagining first in the *sociocultural* challenges, and later the *sociopolitical* or interactive (cooperative and competitive) ones, that human children face at distinct stages of their ontogeny. As for the roots of pretend-

ing and imagining, and likely other intellectual faculties, my
inquiry finds them in abilities that evolved independently—
again, for a variety of sociocultural and sociopolitical reasons
specific to human childhood. The reasons and roots for pretending and imagining are subsumed under the notion of *grounds*.
Modern human ontogeny is where the grounds for mindvaulting can be found. This explains the book's subtitle.

Mental rehearsals of a unique sort, which I construe as mental
projections of further *mental* states and the actions these states
may generate, are what bring together the various abilities that
animate mindvaulting, in an adaptive response to the sociocultural and sociopolitical pressures of human ontogeny. I call
them "metamental rehearsals." Metamental rehearsals are the
formative matrices and ontogenetic incubators of pretending,
imagining, and other intellectual faculties. The different and
versatile forms as well as expressions that the exercise of these
faculties take in childhood and adulthood result from the initial
schemes for metamental rehearsals connecting later with other
capabilities, such as conceptual networks, forms of memory,
language, imagery, and so on. These new connections respond
to various new domains and areas of interest, beyond the formative ones, that increasingly engage the developing intellect, like
branches growing out of the initial roots.

Putting all the metaphors and previewed notions together,
pretending and imagining can be said to be the major forms of
mindvaulting that catapult young minds toward the arched roof
of the intellect, as a result of and in response to the unique,
persistent, and intensely sociocultural and sociopolitical pressures of modern human childhood.

This book continues a series of earlier (mostly) book-length
inquiries into the sociocultural grounds (roots and reasons)

of several uniquely human competencies, such as intuitive psychology, reflexive thinking, predicative thinking, and self-consciousness. The reactions of many people over the years (students, other audiences, reviewers, and discussion partners) to presentations of this wider and long-term research program must have been imperceptibly and hence namelessly sublimated in some of the ideas pursued in this book. More perceptible and hence attributable, with warm thanks, are the questions and comments of audiences of students and colleagues at two consecutive summer seminars in 2010 and 2011 at the University of Bucharest, and those of Dan Dennett, Mircea Dumitru, Gyorgy Gergely, Nick Humphrey, Pierre Jacob, and Dan Sperber, who heard a small fragment of what follows at the memorable workshop inaugurating the Open Mind program at the University of Bucharest in June 2011.

I offer a second round of heartfelt thanks to four anonymous reviewers of the manuscript, for their excellent comments and suggestions, and particularly the one whose extensive, encouraging, and stimulating remarks about this book along with my work in general made me feel like a honorary developmental psychologist, despite my obvious limitation to armchair cogitation.

Finally, I am grateful to the wonderful MIT Press colleagues—senior editor Phil Laughlin, assistant editor Katie Persons, production editor Deborah Cantor-Adams, and copy editor Cindy Milstein—who turned a long-labored manuscript into an elegant book with utmost professionalism, dedication, and good cheer.

I dedicate this book to my beloved Catalina, whose unparalleled imagination has blessed her wonderful art—sampled on the covers of all my MIT Press books—as it has blessed our life together.

Introduction

Although grounded biologically in immediate motivation, perception, emotion, and action, the human mind is also capable, often at the same time, of engaging in such high-level mental activities as reasoning, deliberate planning, thoughtful communication, reflective problem solving and decision making, art creation, technological innovation, and scientific theorizing. I group all these high-level pursuits under the label of *intellect*. What is most characteristic about and central to the work of the intellect is its capacity to vault itself consciously as well as deliberately out of the realm of current perception, motivation, emotion, and action, and leap over to future, past, abstract, possible, or even impossible facts, situations, or scenarios. Metaphorically, as noted in the preface, I call this capacity mindvaulting and distinguish two versions of it: pretending and imagining. The latter I construe as the engine of the intellect.

My inquiry starts, in chapter 1, with two major evolutionary puzzles about mindvaulting and by implication the intellect. The first major puzzle is the phylogenetic uniqueness of human mindvaulting, with no known parallels or precursors in animal minds. The second major puzzle is why mindvaulting evolved at all. For, I will argue, it isn't obvious what selection pressures promoting survival and reproductive fitness might have brought about mindvaulting and, again, by implication an intellect.

Imagination, as the chief form of mindvaulting, has some properties, such as domain versatility, nonmodularity, and significant variability of use, that resist standard evolutionary explanations. This resistance is confirmed by a suite of more concrete puzzles—historical, neuropsychological, genetic, and developmental—that converge on the conjecture that imagination (and by implication the intellect) does not look like a "mental organ" (or sum of such organs) whose properties express structural genes installed gradually by natural selection in response to pressures directly impinging on survival and reproductive fitness.

The way out of this set of puzzles, I conjecture, is to reorient the inquiry toward modern human ontogeny, construed as an environment of evolution sui generis, with its unique selection pressures as well as adaptive responses to such pressures. Mindvaulting and the intellect are outcomes of a unique ontogeny, which must be reanalyzed in a new paradigm of developmental evolution, or for short, *devo-evo*.

According to chapter 2, such a reanalysis points to the persistent and decisive impact of sociocultural and later sociopolitical pressures during early and midchildhood on the development of mindvaulting, first as pretending and later as imagining. These powerful pressures call for appropriate mental competencies as adaptive responses.

After disposing of various misconceptions about imagination, usually pitched at the level of outputs or performances, chapter 3 proposes competencies for metamental rehearsals as the sources and operational core of both pretending and imagining. The rehearsals are called metamental because they involve mental projections that explicitly project further mental states. In evolutionary terms, the metamental rehearsal capacity running online pretend play between the ages of two and four develops primarily to handle sociocultural learning, whereas the metamental rehearsal capacity running offline imagining after age four develops mainly to handle (what I will call) sociopolitical strategizing.

Pretending and imagining are versions of mindvaulting because both engage in conscious, deliberate, and effortful metamental rehearsals that treat one's own thoughts as tool-like means to ends. It is this tool-like treatment of thoughts in the metamental rehearsals of those formative years that best explains how children manage the escalating sociocultural and sociopolitical challenges of their ontogeny, and why and how, in the process, they become imaginative and grow an intellect.

As initial matrices and incubators of pretending and imagining, the metamental rehearsals that run cultural learning and strategizing recruit as well as integrate, or (in a word) assemble, a variety of available or precursor abilities—which I call *foundations*—that develop initially for a variety of reasons in a variety of domains, ranging from projection, imitation, and naive psychology in early childhood, to new executive abilities and a metarepresentational commonsense psychology in later childhood. Chapters 4 and 6 introduce and survey the foundations of pretending and imagining, respectively.

Dissenting from a rather wide consensus in the psychological literature, I do not see pretending as developing organically into imagining and hence the intellect. As chapter 5 explains, pretending is a dated ontogenetic adaptation that responds to dated sociocultural challenges of early childhood. At the same time, in doing its dated job, pretending also creates some of the premises for the later but largely independent development of imagination, which responds to a distinct and later emerging set of sociopolitical challenges. So construed, pretending is, in biological jargon, a preadaptation for, but not a direct precursor of, imagination: the former helps create some (but not all) of the conditions in which the latter can evolve.

Given that new foundational abilities develop after the age of four, chapter 7 analyzes the grounds—roots and reasons—for offline imagination. It argues that the metamental rehearsals that will mutate into a competence for imagination initially develop to handle the new juvenile sociopolitics (cooperative as well as competitive) of midchildhood and later. The adaptive response is a competence for mental strategizing—the initial matrix and incubator of imagining. The chapter ends with a set of pointers as to why and how the initial matrix of strategizing is likely to morph into imagining.

The book concludes with a brief epilogue that summarizes the whole story, ventures some speculations about how the main plot may have played out in the history of the human species, and reflects on the role of evolution and in particular of its devo-evo version in the cognitive science of intellectual faculties. An appendix further clarifies my take on intuitive psychology as the main architect of mindvaulting, and a glossary helps keep track of the terminology and main explanatory concepts employed in the text.

A caveat before proceeding: the first three chapters set the evolutionary stage, and motivate the framework and tools of my inquiry; they do not directly engage the topics of pretending and imagining. The reader who needs no convincing that modern human ontogeny is subject to its own unique evolutionary forces and produces mindvaulting as a result may proceed to the second part, and sample the first only on a need-to-know basis, particularly the sections (2.3, 2.4, and 3.3) that introduce the main tools of analysis. But that impatient reader will surely miss the evolutionary mystery drama and its intellectual fun.

I QUESTIONS

The first part of this book sets the stage for the story told in the second part. It introduces the main characters, pretending and Imagining, as principal forms of mindvaulting, indicates what is puzzling about them, and explains why only a close evolutionary look at modern human ontogeny along with its sociocultural and sociopolitical coordinates can provide a plausible account of not only the emergence but also the nature and design of mindvaulting—this uniquely human and rather recent form of cognition. This, to put it delicately, is not the prevailing view in philosophy, psychology, and cognitive science in general, in part because the larger evolutionary stage, as set up here, is rarely informing the most popular lines of inquiry. (I return to this matter in the epilogue.) During this process of stage setting, the main tools of my analysis will also be introduced and motivated.

As far as I can see, there is a great deal at stake in setting up the larger evolutionary stage and setting it up right. For I take imaginative mindvaulting to be the heart of the unique human intellect, and the latter to have an unusual and surprising evolution. These two aspects, which (alongside language) define what is essential and unique about the modern human mind, transcend in importance the disagreements about the operational details of pretending and imagining as well as the details of their emergence. Those details will occupy the second part of the book. The deeper and more challenging evolutionary background, however, is sketched in this first part.

1 What Sort of Evolution?

Aside from language, there is a suite of higher mental faculties that is puzzling from an evolutionary perspective. It encompasses reasoning, deliberate planning, thoughtful communication, reflective decision making and problem solving, art creation, and scientific theorizing. As noted, I group the competencies involved under the term of intellect, and call their individual deployments intellectual activities. This book aims to explore the common ground of these diverse competencies and activities. This, I suggest, is the capacity to form and deploy thoughts about nonactual, possible, future, or counterfactual scenarios in a deliberate, self-conscious, effortful, reflective, and introspectively active form of offline processing of information. So construed, this capacity can be said to be the engine of the intellect.

With some trepidation, I call this capacity *Imagination*. The trepidation is caused by the rather wild versatility of the notion of Imagination, sampled in chapter 3. For now, it suffices to stress that my inquiry is solely concerned with Imagination as a core competence of the intellect. It is Imagination with a capital *I*, often called productive, reflective, or suppositional Imagination. In chapter 3, I argue that other alleged forms of imagination—imagination with a small *i*—are actually precursors or limited expressions of only some of the mental abilities that run Imagination (in the strong sense adopted here). As a starting point, section 1.1 draws an intuitive profile of key abilities that form the competence for Imagination. Section 1.2 surveys a host of evolutionary puzzles surrounding these abilities. Several standard explanations of the puzzles, examined in section 1.3, are found unsatisfactory. The evolutionary explanation I favor, elaborated in section 1.4, points to human ontogeny as a genuine source of and space for mental evolution, with its specific pressures and adaptive responses. It is the uniqueness and (likely) recency of the modern human ontogeny along with its unique evolutionary parameters that can plausibly explain the uniqueness and recency of mindvaulting in general, Imagination, and hence the intellect itself in particular.

1.1 Intuitive Debut

I am planning our next vacation. Where should we go? On the familiar side, I recruit from memory, and deploy mental images of places visited and liked in the past; I mentally image myself walking on cobbled streets or grand boulevards, lunching with friends and just enjoying nonintellectual bliss. On the nonimagistic and less familiar side, I recall descriptive information about new places, combine it with what I read or find on the Web, make comparisons between the two sets, according to some criteria (say, pleasure, novelty, effort, and cost), produce some evaluations, and reason to some provisional conclusions. A discussion with my dearest gets me to change my perspective (as it often does), adopt hers, and reexamine the choices. A new brainstorming follows along similar lines. I will spare the reader the rest, as it is rather familiar to most people. Countless choices, decisions, and plans are Imaginatively thought through daily by people in similarly mixed imagistic, descriptive, and inferential patterns.

It all looks simple, natural, and easy. And it is, once the competence is fully installed. But it isn't so simple, natural, and easy if we look at the matter from a historical, evolutionary, developmental, and animal-comparative perspective, as I will throughout this book. To begin to see why it isn't, I will take a quick intuitive look at the key mental abilities involved in such exercises of Imagination. To mark their collective contribution to the competence for Imagination, I will call them *I-abilities*.

list of I-abilities

• deliberately positing a goal

• mental playfulness

• deliberate offline projection of various scenarios, often independently of current perceptual inputs, needs, and motives

• quarantining the activity and content of projections from concurrent perception and action

• active and flexible manipulation of the projective thoughts

• metacognitively monitoring and controlling the projective thoughts deployed in the pursuit of a goal

• suppositionally taking (or mentally adopting and inhabiting) the perspective of what is projected and deploying further thoughts (imagistic or abstract) from that perspective

• content promiscuity, in the sense that the Imaginer can deliberately access, mix, and coordinate different kinds of inputs and representations (images, abstract thoughts, gestures, or word meanings) from a variety of sources and mental modalities

• active and deliberate recall of memory items

• thematic connectivity, in the sense that what is projected echoes—or deliberately violates—recognizable or intelligible patterns or scripts of activity and sequences of states of affairs normally encountered in real life

• an understanding and awareness that one's projective thoughts are directed at or represent targets of interest (i.e., self-directed metarepresentation)

• projection of a possible, past, or future self (distinct from the current self who projects), with its possible, past, or future mental states in some possible, past, or future worlds

There are of course other—collateral or enabling—abilities associated with the exercise of Imagination, such as language, concepts, imagery, and more, but the I-abilities just listed are surely constitutive and thus essential. I propose to treat the latter as the *core infrastructure* of Imagining, or what makes it a distinct competence. Pursuing the leading metaphor of mind-vaulting, we can think of this core infrastructure as a supporting device—such as a mental pole—that enables the mind to vault itself into fantasized, anticipated, past, future, or possible worlds. In actual pole vaulting, how high and far one vaults oneself, in what direction, and with what impact and effects all depend on a host of enabling physical and mental abilities. Yet without the pole, there would be no vaulting. Likewise, actual mindvaulting draws on a variety of enabling or collateral mental resources, narrowly linguistic as well as generally representational, infer-ential, and executive, which all impact on the quality, range, and effectiveness of one's Imagining. Without the core infra-structure as a mental pole, however, there would be no mind-vaulting in the first place. It is the pole (hence the core infrastructure) that is universal in human minds, whereas the enablers are likely to produce variability in the exercise of Imagination.

The theoretical conundrum posed by the core infrastructure of Imagining—and by implication the intellect—is that almost all of its component abilities are puzzling from a standard evolutionary perspective. The next section begins to explain why.

1.2   An Assortment of Puzzles

Major puzzles

There are at least two major evolutionary puzzles about Imagination, as I construe it, and the intellect. One is *phylogenetic uniqueness*. Imagination is uniquely human, with (so far) no known versions in other primate and animal species. Imagination may also be rather recent even in the history of humans. Why this uniqueness and (probable) recency? I know of no good answer that commands sufficiently wide acceptance among experts.

The other puzzle about Imagination is *why* it evolved in the first place. Surprising as it may sound, it is not obvious what specific adaptive functions Imagination may have had when it first evolved. In other words, it is not obvious what sort of facts in the physical or social environments, or what relations to such environments, could have acted as selection pressures for Imagination—in the way, for example, in which it is fairly obvious what facts in or relations to the physical environment selected for vision or sensorimotor coordination.

Once available, Imagination is put to many new and probably adaptive uses. These uses, such as planning and envisaging long-term projects, may increase the user's overall fitness and thus further explain the persistence of Imagination in human minds. But they cannot, I think, explain why and how Imagination evolved in the first place. Why the I-abilities, and why their joint work? Why would deliberate, reflective planning require metarepresentation, playfulness, or content promiscuity? Perhaps there is simple ape planning, but not deliberate and reflective planning. Isn't it rather the other way around—that deliberate and reflective planning become possible and effective precisely because the I-abilities that run it are already available, for other evolutionary reasons? Another problem with the argument that various adaptive uses explain its evolution is that Imagination is versatile and operates in diverse domains; it is not clear which one or ones *initially* generated the right selection pressures. Did Imagination first evolve in response to challenges in practical action, tool handling, social interaction, or assimilation of culture, or what else? A quick look at the list of I-abilities from the previous section (as well as the discussion in chapter 7) would show that only a few such abilities are shared by Imaginative pursuits in these various domains.

A second and related problem is precisely the domain versatility and apparent nonmodularity of Imagination (and the intellect it runs). These two features are so unlike what natural selection is supposed to install in organisms and their minds— that is, tightly specialized and narrowly focused organs and mechanisms. And a third problem, as work in social-cognitive psychology has shown, is that people are not very good at and actually perform rather poorly in many intellectual activities that draw on Imagination, such as planning, decision making, problem solving, probabilistic reasoning, and counterfactual thinking. People also show marked differences in the use of Imagination: some people, such as artists and scientists, are significantly better than others. How, then, could Imagination be a universal adaptation? And again, an adaptation to what, and in what domains?

Concrete puzzles

These major evolutionary puzzles about Imagination can be reanalyzed in terms of and actually derived from more concrete puzzles—historical, neuropsychological, genetic, and developmental. Since most of these puzzles are fairly familiar, a brief and schematic survey will do. To simplify the exposition, I will refer collectively to the I-abilities listed earlier as Imagination. So here we go.

historical

• Imagination is uniquely human, without known animal precedents, not even among the closest primates, and as the next numbers suggest, it may belong exclusively to modern humans and not even to their archaic ancestors

• from its outputs—in the form of complex tools, artistic depictions and artifacts, and religious and ornamental objects—Imagination may have evolved rather recently, perhaps in the last 150,000 to 100,000 years, or according to some estimates, even as recently as 70,000 to 50,000 years ago; this would be significantly later than the presumed evolution of language and the basic design of the modern human brain (Boyd and Silk 1997; Coolidge and Wynn 2009; Klein with Edgar 2002; Mithen 1996)

neuropsychological

• there seem to be no specialized or dedicated brain sites for Imagination

• Imagination is domain inspecific, informationally versatile, and cognitively open and penetrable

• Imagination is less prone to neural breakdown, malfunction, and aging than specialized cognitive mechanisms, such as vision, memory, or sensorimotor coordination

• in short, Imagination does not seem to operate as a mental module, in the Fodorian sense of a functionally specialized, domain-specific, hardwired, and brain-localized mechanism (Fodor 1983), as the next set of data also suggest

genetic

• modern humans and chimpanzees are thought to share around 96 percent or perhaps more of their structural genome— that is, the set of genes whose expressions build tissues, organs, and in particular brains

• it is likely that the structural genomes of early Homo lineages and ours may have overlapped even more, yet we Homo sapiens can Imagine, and they probably didn't or only did so to a limited extent

• one can infer from these comparisons that Imagination is unlikely to be encoded in and transcribed from the structural genes of the primate or even shared hominid genome

• adding the neuropsychological facts cited earlier, one can infer that Imagination is unlikely to be innately programmed into the brain

• and yet Imagination is universal in normal humans (although exercised variably) and develops in childhood according to a rather well-paced schedule, though not in the ways that other bodily and mental abilities develop, as the next set of puzzles suggests *developmental*

• most of the I-abilities critically involved in the construction and operation of Imagination are composites made of further abilities, some of which are composed of still further abilities; what is puzzling is that at each level of composition, many component abilities are ontogenetic adaptations in their own right, with well-defined functions and domains that are different from those of the resulting composites

• the implication is that the developing architecture of Imagination is made of many independent I-abilities (listed earlier) that do not mature out of a common core in the structural genome, initially have a proprietary domain and functional life of their own, and would probably not interact and become interdependent as Imagination unless pressured to play new, compelling roles that cannot be adaptively played otherwise

1.3 Possible Explanations

As I see it, the facts, estimates, and numbers just surveyed add up to a rather significant departure from the standard conception of evolution that joins Darwin's theory of natural selection and structural genetics. The standard conception views natural selection as operating on variable traits that express structural genes; in the mental domain, it sees evolution as installing specialized mechanisms as mental organs or modules. Yet according to the evidence sampled so far, this conception cannot explain plausibly the evolution of Imagination. The latter does not look like a mental organ of the standard sort. So the question is, How else could Imagination enter modern human minds and possibly these minds alone, by what route?

Implausible candidates

One possibility is *genetic mutations* of the sort contemplated by Noam Chomsky (1988) to explain the sudden emergence of grammar or by paleoanthropologist Robert Klein (2002) to explain the rewiring of the modern brain about fifty thousand years ago—a rewiring that Klein deems responsible for the dawn of modern human culture. Neither Chomsky nor Klein go into the details of what sort of genes are involved, but we may assume that they mean specialized structural genes. After all, Chomsky frequently talks of grammar as a mental organ, and Klein talks of the spoken phonemic language as the most critical result of the mutation: the sort of mental traits that express structural genes. In the same vein, Frederick Coolidge and Thomas Wynn (2009) envisage a single mutation responsible for a capacious working memory that made a mighty difference to modern representational and computational powers.

But if structural genes are involved, it is hard to see how *just one single* mutation could have led to such a complex competence as grammar or more widely language (Pinker and Bloom 1990; Dennett 1991), let alone a diverse battery of I-abilities, with the domain versatility and nonmodular properties surveyed earlier, and developing at different stages of childhood. Even if one or more mutations may have started the process, as they often do, what finally matters are the selection pressures that may have spread and maintained the new acquisitions in the population of modern humans. But as noted, it is not obvious what those selection pressures were.

Could *learning*, individual or social, provide an alternative explanation of the origins of Imagination? Not likely, I think, for several reasons. How would one learn to Imagine (or in terms of intellectual activities, make decisions, reason, or think about one's own thoughts)? What could be the possible models or examples out there to be copied, emulated, imitated, or generalized from—the utterances of others, their actions or bodily postures?

And how to account for the universality of Imagination and its fairly well-paced sequential development, when (outside simple associations) learning depends on many variables, such as variable challenges and environments as well as differences in talent, energy, motivation, sensory inputs, and so on, which usually lead to variable outcomes at different times in different people?

If Imagination does not mature out of a structural genome, and is not learned from experience either, how else could it enter the minds of modern humans—our minds? Is there another explanation? I think there is, and it is a genuine evolutionary explanation. But it will require some footwork to articulate and defend it.

The developmental alternative

Here is a preview of how I propose to explain the puzzling Imagination:

step 1 Imagination has no apparent precedents in animal species; it is not a specialized mental organ developing out of dedicated structural genes, yet it is universal in design and development

step 2 all this suggests genetic factors at work, some nonstructural, which respond to selection pressures that do not leave structural traces in the genome

step 3 so there must be some form of selection acting on something that is uniquely human and develops in uniquely human ways; what could *that* unique target of selection be?

hypothesis   the answer that stares at us—at me, for one—is the *ontogeny* of modern humans, with its unique selection forces and equally unique adaptive responses to it, particularly in the mental domain

more specifically   Imagination is likely to be an outcome of human ontogeny, but not in the familiar terms of nature or nurture, or the interaction between the two; the specieswide universality of the I-abilities involved in Imagining and their tightly scheduled ontogenesis suggest genetic factors at work, but not of a structural or organ-building nature, and hence probably not in response to pressures directly affecting *physical* survival and *reproductive* fitness

The first step in unpacking this hypothesis is to describe the action of evolution on ontogeny, which is what the next section does.

1.4 Evolutionary Turn to Ontogeny

As scientific background for the entire project, the first order of business is to ascertain that human ontogeny is indeed a legitimate territory as well as target of evolution, that unique selection pressures during ontogeny acting on specific developmental processes can lead to unique adaptive responses, and that this ontogeny-driven selection operates on nonstructural genes as well as epigenetic interactions. Together, these ideas go some way toward unpuzzling many of the puzzles listed earlier in section 2.

Recentering the evolutionary analysis on ontogeny goes against the traditional view of ontogeny as merely the road to reproductive adulthood. I call this traditional view *finalistic* because it takes the capacities that emerge in childhood as being for or for the sake of the final adult phenotype. At least with respect to the capacities involved in the ontogenesis of Imagination, this is the wrong view, for several reasons that are detailed next.

I introduce this recentering on ontogeny by recalling a basic evolutionary syllogism: ontogeny *should* be understood in evolutionary terms because the forces of selection operate on phenotypes, not genotypes, and genotypes *become* phenotypes during ontogeny. In other words, the work of selection forces is done through, during, and on development. I propose to unpack this evolutionary syllogism in three steps that closely reflect its meaning. The first two steps are about selection *through* and *during* development. The third step, concerned with selection acting *on* development, will be at the heart of my argument.

First step: Evo-devo
Ontogenetic trajectories and their underlying developmental programs, rather then adult traits, are selected in evolution. This is to say that novelties in adult traits result from novelties in ontogenetic trajectories, which in turn are caused by changes in the ontogenetic environments along with the selection pressures that these environments and their changes generate.

This is the angle of evolutionary developmental biology, or *evo-devo*, in short. This notion tells us that the development of phenotypes depends on *regulatory genes* turning on and off structural genes at different times and sites during development. Evolutionary changes in regulatory genes lead to different structural genes being expressed or shut off at different times as well as in different interactions, thus resulting in a diversity of phenotypes (Carroll 2005).

It turns out that regulatory genes are not the only mechanisms acting on and modifying the expression of the structural genome during development. Bits of RNA, proteins, and molecules surrounding a given cell and its DNA, acting as *epigenetic markers*, are also involved in transcribing and transferring genetic information. Heredity, to put it another way, operates both with DNA and epigenetic mechanisms. Epigenetic inheritance is directly relevant to this discussion for two reasons: first, it may involve changes in DNA expression and its timing *without* changes in the DNA sequences themselves; and second, both regulatory genes and epigenetic markers, which together control most of DNA expression from a largely *nonstructural* platform, tend to reflect an organism's *environmental* conditions and changes in such conditions, including selection pressures (Michel 2010). The stability of the epigenetic environment may explain the stability and durability of epigenetic inheritance, which in turn may explain the stability and durability of mental traits emerging outside the reach of the structural genome. This latter environmental implication leads to the next step in my argument.

Second step: Eco-devo

Another recent paradigm in evolutionary theory is so-called ecological developmental biology, or *eco-devo* (Michel 2010). The basic idea of eco-devo is that information in the genome is *functionally* intertwined with ecological influences at different stages of development, in the sense that reliable and recurrent features of external stimulation and experience at a stage constitute a sort of "ontogenetic niche" that is inherited together with the genome (West and King 1987; Lickliter and Harshaw 2010). As a result, changes in ontogenetic niches and their sequencing, reflected in selection pressures, can bring about changes in behavioral strategies and other phenotypic traits, leading to new organism-environment relations. Two critical questions arise at this point. A general question is what explains how new organism-environment relations end up in new ontogenetic trajectories. A narrower question—central to this book—is what historically led to changes in ontogenetic niches, and what new selection pressures originating in the new ontogenetic niches caused the development of mind-vaulting in general, and pretending, Imagining, and other intellectual faculties in particular.

Before tackling these issues, I note, as an interlude, that the first two steps, evo-devo and eco-devo, *already* begin to explain some of the puzzles evoked in section 1.2.

Unpuzzling some puzzles

The leading evolutionary-cum-genetic puzzle was the 96 percent or so overlap of the ape and human structural genome, but the huge differences in mental capabilities. The evo-devo and eco-devo accounts suggest that the reason for the differences is likely found in the particulars of human ontogeny. Evo-devo also predicts that mental differences between modern humans and apes—as well as possibly between modern and archaic humans—are likely to originate in regulatory genes and epigenetic markers operating during development, without leaving many, if any, structural traces in the genome. The result may well be new mental abilities that lack their own structurally dedicated genetic bases.

Specifically, evolutionary changes in regulatory genes and epigenetic markers may explain the 96 percent structural genome shared by apes and modern humans in contrast with the unshared Imagination (and an intellect more generally). It turns out that many structural genes expressed in humans are not expressed in apes, and this difference affects mostly the brain (Preuss et al. 2004). Similar regulatory and epigenetic changes are thought to have led to a dramatic extension of human childhood in general, the delay of puberty, the dramatic mental changes in the age five to seven interval (which I will explore further in chapter 6), and the novelty of human adolescence—all of which have major and novel mental consequences (Konner 2010).

These, of course, are general implications. What remains to be explained is how regulatory genes and epigenetic markers manage to effect such developmental changes, and why. One can only hope that such an explanation will be forthcoming one day.

The other paradigm, eco-devo, can be brought into the picture at this juncture, since it posits that changes in ontogenetic niches—from those of apes to those of archaic and then modern humans—most likely impacted regulatory genes and epigenetic markers, which in turn may have led to new mental abilities. Understanding the nature and scope of this impact requires taking the third and crucial step in this brief metaevolutionary survey.

Third step: Devo-evo

The moral so far is that ontogeny has an evolutionary life of its own, complex and multidimensional. To capture its impact on mental development, I suggest we need a third paradigm: developmental evolutionary theory, or what I baptized early as devo-evo. This paradigm tracks mental development along a sequence of ontogenetic niches, each with its own selection pressures, to which young minds develop responses as ontogenetic adaptations and solutions. So viewed, many abilities involved in the emergence and operation of pretending and Imagining—along with the intellect more generally and other unique human acquisitions—would appear as outcomes of selection for ontogenetic adaptations as well as solutions and their developmental trajectories. Let us take a closer look at these evo-devo parameters.

Ontogenetic adaptations and solutions

Talk of adaptation, particularly in the mental domain, is bound to be controversial and open to misunderstanding, so I will keep things as simple and consensual as possible, and geared only to what matters to the present inquiry.

The relatively recent concept of *ontogenetic adaptation* is intended to capture those traits that serve specific adaptive functions for the developing organism in response to specific and usually dated pressures in niches specific to distinct developmental stages (Oppenheim 1981). Ronald Oppenheim's standard example is that of the metamorphosis of a tadpole into a frog. Both tadpole and frog are well adapted to their habitat: the tadpole is well adapted to its aquatic environment and the need to breathe in water, and the frog is well adapted to its terrestrial existence and need to breathe in air.

In the cognitive domain, one instance of ontogenetic adaptation is the ability of neonates to respond spontaneously to the intensity-based equivalence of auditory and visual inputs—an ability lost in adulthood. Even though neonates exhibit an early intersensory integration, they cannot make other, higher-level types of intersensory integration, which older children and adults can. This early ability to perceive intensity-based inter-

sensory equivalence provides neonates an adaptively meaningful way to begin to learn about the perceptual unity of their
world in a "buffered" and measured way (Marcovitch and
Lewkowicz 2004). Another early cognitive example is that of the
imitation of facial expressions by newborns, which peters out
around two months (Bjorklund and Pellegrini 2001, 38). A
further and much more complex case that will take an entire
chapter to examine (chapter 5 below) is that of pretend play,
active between ages two and four.

Ontogenetic adaptations are universal—all normal newborns
or young children display the abilities just illustrated—and may
indicate a long past history of selection. In some contrast, what
I call *ontogenetic solution* is an ability that responds adaptively
to dated pressures and may have long-term benefits, but shows
some variability among individuals as well as in the timing of
its development, and suggests a pattern of assembly out of pre-
existing abilities that may have had independent function for
independent reasons. The assembly also works for ontogenetic
adaptations, but in a more uniform and constrained way than
for ontogenetic solutions.

More clearly than ontogenetic adaptations, ontogenetic solutions lack a dedicated genetic basis and most often dedicated brain
sites, and are more likely to respond to selection forces of a social
and cultural sort. Metaphorically speaking, ontogenetic solutions
emerge because all the right ingredients are available and fall into
the right pattern under the right conditions and pressures, particularly if (as in human ontogeny) the pattern in question is
sufficiently constrained by adult interactions and their culture.

The third feature of ontogenetic solutions, assembly, is critical to the argument about Imagination presented here (and

other mental traits unique to humans; Bogdan 1997, 2000, 2009, 2010). Stanislas Dehaene's excellent *The Number Sense* provides a good intuitive feel for the notion of ontogenetic assembly. Dehaene notes that "the number sense is the patchwork of multiple core processes," and the concept of a natural number arises from the capacity to track a small number of objects (up to three), combined with our intuitive number sense, which tells us that any set, however large, has a cardinal number. "Somehow, around the age of 3 or 4, the two systems snap together" (Dehaene 1997/2011, 257, 260). The road is open to higher abstract mathematics. Dehaene's "snapping together" is close to my notion of assembly.

Dehaene does not speculate about the reasons for the arithmetic snapping together, yet is emphatic that it "is not automatic and somehow triggered by the maturation of the human brain. It is a *cultural* invention" (ibid., 260). Reporting research on the arithmetic of Amazonian tribes, Dehaene observes that tribe members are competent with approximate numbers, but lack a sense of exact numbers—that is, a counting system. The latter, interestingly, must be *symbolic*, in the sense of having items (words, points on the body, abacus units, and tally marks) uniquely representing numbers and being recognized as such. Some form of metarepresentation must therefore be involved. (Helpful fingers apparently fail to metarepresent.) One can infer from here that in the early ontogeny of modern non-Amazonian children, the cultural practice of and hence pressure for exact counting recruits the more basic as well as historically older competence for approximate counting and some symbolic system of unique numerical reference, and snaps them together in an assembled composite.

So construed, I take the number sense to be an ontogenetic *solution* that responds adaptively to the cultural pressures of childhood, but has long-term benefits, lacks a genetic basis and a long history of natural selection, and thus is not quite universal in the human species. Looking ahead, I conjecture that pretend play is an assembled ontogenetic adaptation as (most probably) is strategizing, the initial matrix of Imagination, but Imagination itself is an ontogenetic solution that further combines and assembles the resources for strategizing along with other enabling and collateral abilities.

Before demonstrating this conjecture in the second part of this book, I should probe further and ask what *inside* children's heads could explain the possibility of such a devo-evo assembly of ontogenetic adaptations and solutions. The following is an answer that I find rather plausible.

A brain for assembly

With different degrees of scope and strength, the empirical evidence converges from several areas. A general evolutionary nod toward assembly is natural selection's propensity to introduce novelty by tinkering with old resources. Assembly is one good way of tinkering. Evidence of it can be found in brain areas that handle multiple although dissimilar task domains, such as action observation and execution, vision, emotion, language, and reasoning. To do so, such brain areas must interact with many other brain areas, and if the interactions crystallize in robust and durable patterns, assembly is likely to be involved. Assembly is also more likely to be involved in the more recently evolved mental competencies rather than older ones. This is because newer competencies are likely to recruit available but widely distributed neural circuits, as is the case with the frontal areas of the human brain, which support such diverse yet recently evolved capabilities as language, reasoning, and mental imagery (Anderson 2010).

Heterochrony is another evolutionary incentive for assembly. In modern humans, it is responsible for dramatic changes in the timing of ontogenetic trajectories, leading to an unprecedentedly long childhood, whose segments themselves are either unusual in the animal world (e.g., an extended and helpless infancy, and the significant delay of puberty) or entirely new (the five to seven period, and adolescence). As a result, traits that in apes or archaic humans had a given developmental functionality in a given period, are maintained in modern children beyond that period, thereby enabling them to interact with later developing traits, producing a variability of new traits on which selection can act and produce new ontogenetic adaptations as well as solutions (West-Eberhard 2003; for the larger picture of the evolution of modern childhood, see also Konner 2010).

It is a familiar idea in evolutionary theory that a lengthy ontogeny increases adaptability by allowing offspring more time, energy, and brain flexibility to adjust to highly complex environments, and in the human case, complex social interactions and the arms-race dynamics of human culture (Bjorklund and Pellegrini 2001). This evolutionary idea is echoed in neuroscience, where the thinking is that by retarding or extending the rate of somatic development, neural structures are given more time to grow and differentiate, and therefore be affected by the developmental milieu. This idea is often taken to imply that neural plasticity is selected for *learning*. That may be true about mental inductions, such as accumulating information along with acquiring behavioral and cultural routines, but probably less true about developing mental abilities, such as acquiring words, thinking abstractly, or Imagining. After all, most animal species learn in the former sense but do not develop the latter abilities, not even among nonhuman primates with a lengthy childhood.

In the case of children's mental development and its intellectual by-products, neural plasticity may also mean something else. It may mean an evolved *readiness to assemble* task-specific ontogenetic adaptations and solutions out of prior adaptations as well as other already available abilities and dispositions whose initial tasks—and raisons d'être—may have been different. This is how I read the claim that neural development generates redundant and variable synaptic typologies that provide the raw material of epigenesis, so that neural selection, mostly through local and dated pressures, can favor the preservation or stabilization of those synapses that have functional significance in a particular environment at a particular time (Changeux 1985; Dennett 1991). Many mental ontogenetic adaptations and solutions are likely to be outcomes of *selection for an assembly-ready neural plasticity*.

It is within this space of evolutionary opportunities that assembly does its work. But more concretely, how? Work in progress in neuropsychology provides some promising clues. In a wide-ranging survey, Michael Anderson examines several theories that support the notion of assembly introduced here. These are theories of "neural reuse" that "suggest that neural circuits established for one purpose are commonly exapted (exploited, recycled, redeployed) during evolution or normal development, and put to different uses, often without losing their original functions" (2010, 246). Stanislas Dehaene (1997/2011) puts forth one of these theories, called "neuronal recycling," in relation to the ontogenesis of arithmetic. As noted above, Dehaene explicitly construes recycling as assembly, at least in the case of children's naive arithmetic.

Assembly by recycling, but also by other means of neural redeployment, is particularly relevant to the development of pretending and Imagining, because it may produce those modern mental competencies that had not had enough evolutionary time to evolve specialized and rigidly hardwired neural circuits as modules—the implication of some puzzles listed in section 1.2—but had evolved to handle adaptively recent sociocultural tasks in recent ontogenetic niches.

With this general picture of the evolutionary and neural opportunities for the assembly of ontogenetic adaptations along with solutions in the mental and particularly mindvaulting domain, I will take a closer look next at the ontogenetic niches and pressures that turn these opportunities into mental reality in modern children.

2 What Sort of Ontogeny?

What is it about human childhood that could explain the emergence of unique mental traits and in particular Imagination as engine of the intellect? A useful and illuminating explanatory strategy, pursued in section 2.1, is to step back in primate evolution and ask what it is about some apes in human captivity that might explain their unusual mental accomplishments. The answer in section 2.2 points to a deep, intense, and constant immersion and active participation in, and hence assimilation of, some of the sociocultural practices of humans. As little primates in sociocultural captivity, human children share the same condition, which I label *sociocultural activism*. The sociocultural environment makes for a unique ontogeny whose unprecedented challenges call for a unique sort of thoughts—thoughts about mental states employed as means toward ends. So argues section 2.3. According to section 2.4, intuitive psychology is most responsible for such unique thoughts, and to that extent is the driving force behind the development of mindvaulting.

2.1 The Ape Connection

Why would an animal or human mind Imagine? I will have occasion to note (in the next chapter) that there are other ways—simpler, routine, and reflex—that animal minds use to anticipate or predict nonactual situations, or expect them in the future. Why, then (for all we know), would only human minds evolve a capacity to Imagine?

The lessons of cultural captivity

Human culture impacts the minds of nonhuman primates (and probably most captive or domesticated animals as well). Chimpanzees and bonobos in human captivity engage in forms of learning, rudimentary behavior emulation, protosymbolic communication, more advanced tool use, and social cognition that are not observed in the wild—not regularly anyway (Tomasello and Call 1997). These novel behaviors are therefore likely to draw on innovative uses and possibly new combinations of existing abilities. Why these novelties, and what can they tell us about the evolution of the modern human mind and its Imaginative powers in particular? Some preliminary footwork is needed before tackling these questions.

We can distinguish three levels of cultural captivity for nonhuman primates, in an order that reflects the degree of their social, communicational, and cultural involvement with humans. The first level, of lowest involvement, is that of the zoo. The second level, of higher involvement, is that of the research environments in which nonhuman primates live, interact with humans, are systematically observed and trained for various tasks, and perform experiments. The third level, of the highest involvement, is that of adoption and growth in a human family (human reared or homegrown).

The most enculturated apes are the human-reared ones, as part of the family, or the ones, like Kanzi, who grow up in a research setting in close interactions with humans and their cultural habits and gadgets. It is these intensely enculturated apes that become capable of novel cultural behaviors, from apparent pretend play to protosymbolic communication. One may reasonably assume that new uses of existing mental skills are responsible for these cultural novelties in the behavioral repertoire of enculturated apes and possibly dolphins.

The obvious question, then, is, What is it about the novel cultural environments, particularly at levels two and three, that would drive the development of such new uses of mental skills in captive apes (and captive dolphins)? And can the answer tell us something instructive about human childhood, which after all is also a form of cultural captivity?

Parameters of ape enculturation

Viewed through the eyes of captive apes, human culture displays *utter novelty* in its weirdness and unnatural arbitrariness, in homes as well as experimental settings. Novelty, of course, is not enough. Animals can get conditioned to novelty. Unlike pigeons in large, noisy, and hectic cities, or domesticated cats and dogs facing strange household habits, the apes may be further puzzled by bipeds who somehow look and often move like them, yet engage in such weird actions on such weird objects in such weird settings.

The cultural novelty is dramatized by the fact that it occurs in *several domains*, often at once. The domains could be material culture (tools, habitats, and artifacts), food handling (acquisition, processing, and consumption), communication, pedagogy, and social interactions. To get a banana or go out, for example, Kanzi had to type specific lexigrams on the keyboard, and then look at and interact in other ways with the human observer—a cultural behavior spanning several domains (Savage-Rumbaugh and Lewin 1996). Simple and domain-specific associations are not likely to work here.

A third parameter, also obvious in Kanzi's requests, is the *sociocultural interactivity* among the participants. This is not like the sociopolitical games that apes are so good at in the wild or even a zoo. It is rather an act-and-react pattern involving humans *and* their cultural behaviors and artifacts. This is to say that when humans react or communicate in a certain way, the apes must mentally factor in not only the physical, emotional, and behavioral aspects of the human reaction or message but also their cultural implications, concerning, say, the artifacts, action patterns, or tasks involved. Handling such various forms of sociocultural interactivity is not only beyond simple learning by association but actually requires blending several mental skills as well, initially adapted to separate and isolated domains of natural or social behavior.

Finally, these patterns of sociocultural interactivity normally do not stay put, or show up in isolation or randomly. Their *interplay* is not only *dynamic* and often fast changing but also may be *sequenced* according to its own cultural *rules*. If Kanzi wants to go out to play with tools (already a cultural habit), he must communicate lexigrammatically with the human handler, notice the handler's reaction and approval, wait for the handler to open the door, then exit and behave properly, according to the cultural scripts involved. From the moment the desire for play makes itself manifest, Kanzi must activate, combine, and sequence mental skills that respond to this orderly sequence of cultural moves, alternated with social and communicational interactions with humans.

Needless to say, nothing remotely similar occurs in the wild. Even though drawing on mental resources evolved over millions of years in the wild, the young enculturated apes improvise new solutions to new problems, both without precedent in the wild. The tasks and pressures as well as penalties and rewards of enculturation suggest that new mental and behavioral *solutions* are required, for which there are no dedicated genetic predispositions. What is a truly remarkable but ultimately individual and ephemeral improvisation for Kanzi becomes second nature in human children. Unlike Kanzi, human children have had some historical time, over countless generations, to evolve helpful predispositions for the assimilation, mastery, and active manipulation of the sociocultural novelties awaiting them. This is a line of inquiry worth pursuing. So let me take a further step along this route, albeit more speculatively.

What if the minds of young archaic humans initially improvised mental responses to new sociocultural challenges in ways rather similar to those seen in our days in the enculturated homegrown apes? After many trials and errors, the successful improvisations of the early hominid kids may have later turned into second nature, perhaps by genetic assimilation, or at least and more plausibly through a sort of built-in readiness for enculturation—a historical option that the enculturated apes obviously do not have.

What the archaic human parents learned the hard way and imperfectly, perhaps like Kanzi's mother, their young may have assimilated spontaneously and speedily, constantly adding new refinements and improvements. (For an intuitive and instructive parallel, think of how parents and their children today assimilate and handle computers, tablets, and Internet novelties in general. Would future human youngsters develop or retool mental predispositions that are Internet ready, so to speak? That's not impossible, according to current trends.) No wonder, then, that a close look at the parameters of ape ontogenetic enculturation, with such an impact on their minds, shows some parallels to human childhood, and thus opens a window on the reasons for and nature of children's mental adaptations to their sociocultural environments.

With this primate parallel in mind, I now turn to the sociocultural ontogeny of modern human children. For they are constantly facing escalating sociocultural and later sociopolitical challenges that homegrown apes encounter only partially, intermittently, and unnaturally, because occurring across distinct species, and for a limited time anyway.

2.2 Sociocultural Activism

Like Kanzi, human children begin their life as young primates in sociocultural captivity. Their earliest months are spent in massive dependence on adults—the *social* part of their activism. Not quite adept at locomotion and handling physical objects, human infants excel instead at communicating preverbally with adults, registering their intents and emotions, and using them to figure out and reproduce the social and cultural ways in which adults behave and want the infants to behave as well. The later acquisition of language dramatically accelerates this process. It is no exaggeration to say that childhood is a period of intense sociocultural indoctrination (Nelson 1996; Rogoff 1990; Trevarthen 1993, 2011; Tomasello 1999).

It would be hard to find more challenging, intense, and constant mental tasks for human children than those involving the assimilation and mastery of social norms, language, and cultural practices, including uses of tools and other artifacts. A child unable to manage these sociocultural and later sociopolitical tasks is an unadapted child in his early years, yet also unlikely later to marry and leave offspring. It is as basic as that. Beyond childhood, it would be equally hard to find a distinctly human activity that is not infused with and structured by the sociocultural and interpersonal dimensions of life.

As seen in later chapters, Imagining requires a mental machinery that is not only complex but also expensive to maintain and run, especially from the executive stance of inner-directed abilities such as attention, metacognition, metarepresentation, metamental control, and introvert consciousness. There must be good reasons for such a mental machinery to evolve. An Imaginative mind is unlikely to have evolved just to do the physical, biological, and relatively simple sociopolitical and technological chores that other species, and in particular nonhuman primates and archaic humans, could and probably did handle with a simpler mental know-how, widely shared phylogenetically, such as sensorimotor skills, perception and semantic memory, signal communication, some relational thinking, and behavior-sensitive social cognition (Byrne and Whiten 1988; Coolidge and Wynn 2009; Tomasello and Call 1997; Whiten 1991).

Piaget's insights

Registering, assimilating, and reproducing sociocultural practices in childhood are only half the story. Like Kanzi, children not only observe and react to others, and what others do and say, but also operate as willful agents and manipulators, pursuing their goals in sociocultural contexts by acting causally on other people's mental states and actions, and later on their own. This is what the notion of sociocultural activism is all about. I will map out this concept in terms of two remarkable insights of Jean Piaget (1964, 1974).

I think Piaget was importantly right on the crucial link between mental activism and intellect in general, Imagination in particular: it is children's active mental intervention in a domain along with their mental manipulation of targets in that domain that drive the development of intellectual capacities that go beyond perceptual recognition and sensorimotor coordination. Nevertheless, I think Piaget erred in not seeing that the earliest exercises of children's mental agency, with the strongest impact on intellectual development, are socioculturally directed at other people's mental states and actions rather than mechanically directed at physical objects. Piaget also erred in denying an innate head start in recognitional capacities in several domains, including social and communicational ones, which provide an initial platform of predispositions, biases, and developmental constraints for many mental acquisitions later on (Carey 2009; Karmiloff-Smith 1992).

According to later chapters, more basic foundations, such as projection, play, and imitation, alongside intuitive psychology, should be added to this initial platform, if we are to understand from where and why the abilities responsible for pretending as well as Imagining take off. The overall implication is that children's mental agency does not begin its developmental construction of pretending, Imagining, and other intellectual faculties from scratch, and if it begins from some prior platform, it is not that of guiding actions on physical objects.

Piaget had a further and more specific insight about children's mental agency (Piaget 1964, 1974; see also Bogdan 2000, 2010; Tomasello 1999). I will first place this insight into a broader picture. If we think (as we should) of organisms as goal-directed or means–ends systems, we can distinguish at least three kinds of manipulative actions as means to ends. There are actions on items *in* the environment, such as eating, hunting, or mating; there are also actions *with* items of the environment treated as extensions (or implements) of one's body, as in the apes' use of branches to scoop termites or build nests. These two kinds of manipulative actions are practiced by many animals and in particular primate species. Finally, there are actions intended to *cause* some external means, which are independent of one's body and its innate action schemes, to *cause* a desired end. I will refer to this third kind of actions as of the *cause–causation* kind. And rather narrowly, I will call *tools* the means used in cause–causation actions. In other words, means are—or rather become—tools when the means are external, independent, and deliberately caused to cause the desired effects. The implication here, to be elaborated in the next section, is that it takes a specialized *knowledge* of the right properties of the tools employed to achieve the desired effects.

Piaget's second and important insight was that only the mental schemes running cause–causation actions with objects (as tools, on my reading) actually drive the ontogenesis of intellectual capabilities. This is the right insight. But again, it locates the intellect-building actions in a domain of childhood much less consequential for mental development: mechanical actions on physical objects. The focus in what follows is on the more important and consequential social interactions with people and their culture along with the thoughts involved as

mental tools in such interactions. This is the direction of my
argument.

2.3 Unique Ontogeny for Unique Thoughts

As far the ontogenesis of pretending and Imagining as well as
much of the intellect is concerned, it should already be apparent
that the most consequential domains of cause–causation actions
in childhood are initially and primarily sociocultural and sociopolitical. These domains are most likely responsible for a unique
ontogeny with a unique impact on mental development. I will
start with a few words about the uniqueness of human ontogeny
and then add a few more about its impact on the development
of mindvaulting.

Unique ontogeny

Human ontogeny is unique in many ways. I noted a chapter
ago that some of its stages are entirely novel phylogenetically,
the duration of others is unusual, and what happens during
each stage as well as the sequencing of the stages is likely to
have a mighty impact on mental development, including that
of mindvaulting. At the same time, what does not and cannot
happen mentally at a stage, given its specific conditions and
pressures as well as available resources, should guide and con-
strain hypotheses about what mental capabilities are involved,
and how they work.

Human infancy is a potent stimulus for and often incubator
of novel mental abilities, but at first in a somewhat paradoxical
way: the limitations of infancy create unique conditions for
remarkably unusual developments later. Thus, the infants' helplessness and massive adult dependence create stimulative prem-

ises for preverbal yet meaningful communication (in a Gricean sense), and interpersonal relatedness leading to intuitive psychology, collaborative and mutually acknowledged interactions, and word acquisition. All of these are direct or enabling prerequisites for future advances in Imaginative and intellectual abilities (Locke and Bogin 2006; Hobson 1993; Meltzoff and Gopnik 1993; Tomasello 1999; Trevarthen 1993, 2011; see also Bogdan 2000, 2001, 2009).

Among primates, human infancy is also unique in being shorter by at least one year, making room for what seems to be an absolute novelty across animal species—namely, *childhood*—with a tremendous impact on mental development (Locke and Bogin 2006; Konner 2010). Whereas other primates and some archaic humans graduate from infancy directly to juvenility (sexual immaturity but independent survival) and then adulthood, young modern humans spend several interim years setting up and refining their linguistic and intellectual gear, among many other important acquisitions. Extending from around age two and a half to seven, childhood can be viewed as an overall adaptive response to the pressures of assimilating the basics of culture, language, and social life. This assimilation process generates powerful and specific pressures that lead to new mental capacities, including those of pretending, Imagining, and the intellect in general. It is in this sense that those capacities may be viewed as outcomes of modern human childhood. Childhood so construed, as the formative period of mindvaulting, will be in the center of the present inquiry.

Interestingly, adolescence also seems to be a human novelty, and it too appears to make some unique contributions to intellectual development. Whereas childhood is the period during which the *basics* of mindvaulting (pretending and then

Imagining) are set up, adolescence seems to enrich and refine the use of these abilities, particularly of Imagining. Pretend play emerges and is most active in early childhood, between ages two and four or so, whereas Imagining takes off after the four-to-five interval. An analogy with language development can be instructive here: the earliest period two to four is that of acquiring the basics of vocabulary and grammar (words, semantics, and syntax), and the preschool years solidify and expand these acquisitions, but it is only toward the end of the first decade and early adolescence that the pragmatics of language use as discourse begins to be fluently operative (Bruner 1990; Nelson 1996). I think that in the mental domain, Imagining comes close, by analogy, to the pragmatic use of language as discourse, in developmental timing along with what it takes to exercise the competence fully and expertly.

Unique thoughts

To see how the unique human ontogeny impacts on mental development, I propose now to expand my earlier comments on Piaget's insight about cause–causation actions with tool-like mental means employed to reach the desired ends. I suggested above that the Piagetian insight should be recentered on interactions with people and their culture, away from its initial focus on children's actions on physical objects. Against the already-explained background of social life, culture and sociopolitics being the strongest stimuli and shapers of mental development in human childhood, the point I want to make now is that children develop *unique sorts of thoughts* that are at the heart of their mindvaulting—first in pretending and later in Imagining. I will phrase this idea about the uniqueness of such mindvaulting thoughts rather schematically at this early stage, for immediate grasp of its basic content, leaving it for the next chapters to fill in the gaps and add details.

The strong, persistent, and escalating challenges of sociocultural and sociopolitical domains pressure children to engage in mental rehearsals of cause–causation actions and interactions in those domains. Of necessity, these actions and interactions involve other people, and later selves, who cannot be understood, communicated with, and influenced without factoring in their *mental states*. Of necessity, then, children's mental rehearsals in the sociocultural and sociopolitical domains deploy *thoughts about mental states*, of others and later selves, in a cause–causation format. This means that children treat the mental states inhabiting the contents of their thoughts *as tools* that they rehearse in order to pursue their goal strategies. To do that, to treat the mental states they are thinking about *as* tools, children must become cognizant of the relevant properties of mental states in general, primarily their intentionality or aboutness (as philosophers call it), or target directedness (as I prefer to call it), and the causal and functional implications or affordances of those properties. As far as we know, in both pretending and Imagining, the thoughts representing mental states and rehearsing them as tools in the service of one's goal strategies are unique in the armamentarium of animal cognition.

The unique competence responsible for understanding and employing mental states in one's goal strategies is children's developing *intuitive psychology*. The implication should then be clear and unambiguous: no intuitive psychology—no mind-vaulting. Looking ahead, the basic argument that unpacks this implication can be summarized as follows: mental rehearsals originate in the animal brain's basic biological capacity to project memories, action schemes, and experiences, and anticipate courses of action; and such mental rehearsals *become* forms of mindvaulting only in human ontogeny, under unique sociocultural and sociopolitical challenges that can be handled adaptively only by an intuitive psychology that enables children's minds to form thoughts about mental states, and handle them in a cause–causation format as tool-like means to desired ends.

Given the critical role that intuitive psychology plays in the ontogenesis of mindvaulting—a role noted and elaborated throughout this book—I should anticipate my take on this extraordinary competence, for it also informs my stance on the different stages and forms of mindvaulting.

2.4   Intuitive Psychology: The Driving Force

The mental competence I call *intuitive psychology* goes by many other (often misleading) labels, such as theory of mind, mindreading, mentalizing, and folk or commonsense psychology, and is subject to widely different accounts. What matters to the present inquiry is the job of the competence, which is to register, track, represent, and interpret mental states (the cognitive component) and actively employ the results in one's goal strategies (the practical component). For this inquiry, I will select only those features of intuitive psychology that directly affect and shape the development of mindvaulting, leaving to the appendix (and for those interested) a more general exposition and defense of my take on intuitive psychology.

Basics

The domain of intuitive psychology is usually taken to be that of relations between minds, as in empathy, between another mind and the world, as in noticing that somebody sees something, and among two or more minds and the world, as in shared attention. Developmentally, talk of minds as populating the domain of intuitive psychology is a vast simplification, since young children in particular are likely to register others as undivided aggregates of mental and bodily features, or animated or minded bodies, and older children and adults actually interpret mental states on the basis of what is observed, communicated, remembered, read, or inferred.

In figuring out and interpreting mental states, the competence for intuitive psychology is sensitive not only to how those states relate to sundry targets in the world and other minds but also to the *affordances* or *implications*—mental, communicational, or behavioral—of those mind–world, mind–mind, or mind–world–mind relations as grounds for action and intervention. Far from being spectatorial, "theoretical," or merely "simulational," intuitive psychology is eminently practical, forward-looking, interventionist, and interested in as well as shaped by the implications and affordances for action or communication of the mental states it registers, figures out, and reasons about. In other words, intuitive psychology is a practically motivated competence and evolved for this very reason (Bogdan 1997). This critical point, all too frequently neglected in the philosophical and psychological literature, is especially important, because it is the implications and affordances of another person's mental states that normally call for such intuitive-psychological skills as those involved in shared attention, detection of means–ends intentions, perspective taking, and so on. Many of these skills will prove to be indispensable resources for pretending and Imagining.

Three stages, three competencies

I distinguish three major stages in the ontogenesis of intuitive psychology. The competencies involved at each stage vary significantly, but they all share the job of tracking and interpreting mental states along with their affordances for further thought and action. In a first stage, in early infancy, the competence is exercised mostly bilaterally in communication and exchanges of mainly affects, emotions, and intents to interact or socialize (Meltzoff and Moore 1977; Meltzoff and Gopnik 1993; Trevarthen 1993, 2011). This is an extraordinary platform for intuitive psychology, since it provides the infants with an incipient and implicit yet consequential *sense of the mental* (in others), as I call it—a sense of a mental invariant behind various expressions of it (Bogdan 2000, 2001, 2009). A parent, for example, can show happiness (the mental invariant), which the infant detects through its various expressions—singing, lively eyes, smile, exuberant gestures, and so on. I think children inject or factor this sense of mental invariants into the later acquisitions in intuitive psychology, with momentous implications.

In a second stage, older infants and young children until around the age of four also develop a competence to recognize, track, interpret, and react to mostly visible, behaviorally, and communicationally manifested mind–world relations of others, displayed in seeing, attending, simple desires, visually based beliefs, trying to do something, and the like, as well as relations between two or more minds (including one's own) and a shared world, displayed in shared attention and joint action (Astington, Harris, and Olson 1988; Bjorklund 2005; Doherty 2007; Perner 1991; Tomasello 1999; Wellman 1990). I call this competence *naive psychology*, and conjecture that it incorporates and builds on the bilateral sense of the mental developed in the first stage of early infancy (Bogdan 2010).

In a third stage, after the age of four, older children develop the competence to track, interpret, reason about, and react to more complex as well as not always overtly displayed attitudes, such intentions, opinions, hopes, complex emotions, and the like concerning both other people and themselves. I call this competence *commonsense psychology*. Dissenting from a widely shared philosophical and psychological opinion, I think that only older children, after four, can turn their intuitive psychology toward their own minds, and interpret their thoughts and attitudes in the same terms in which they interpret those of others.

To sum up, schematically:

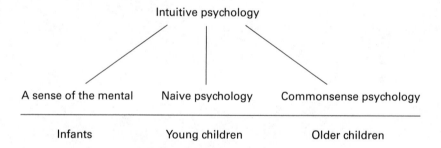

Later chapters (and the appendix) elaborate these distinctions and argue that the intuitive-psychological competencies involved at each stage make distinct contributions to the ontogenesis of mindvaulting. This is to say that the level of expertise in intuitive psychology at a given stage of childhood is bound to shape the level of expertise in handling mental states as tools in children's mental rehearsals and goal strategies, and hence the form and complexity of mindvaulting. In enabling children (and adults) to form thoughts about mental states and employ such thoughts as tool-like means in the pursuit of one's ends, intuitive psychology provides a unique devo-evo recipe for mindvaulting.

How this recipe yields the real mental stuff will be the argument presented in the second part of this book. But in order to tell a plausible story, I need first to disentangle the notions of pretending and particularly Imagining from a perplexing, confusing variety of false or barely qualifying candidates, and then define more closely the competencies involved. This is the business of the next chapter.

3 What Sort of Competence?

It will not be easy to extricate Imagining from the many false candidates that abound in commonsense, philosophical, and psychological conceptions. Yet extricated it must be if we want to understand why and how the heart of the intellect beats as it does. To this end, the first two sections can be regarded as a sort of clearing operation. Section 3.1 breezily surveys some influential philosophical and psychological candidates, and finds a rather messy indeterminacy. Section 3.2 argues that a good deal of the indeterminacy about Imagination reflects an indistinction, if not confusion, between competence and performance, with the latter misleadingly guiding influential insights and theories. This critical exercise is intended not only to separate Imagining from what loosely but confusingly passes as legitimate candidates but also to show that the latter could not possibly be the bases or precursors of the former.

With the competence angle on Imagining thus delineated, section 3.3 construes the defining property of Imagination as deliberately projecting thoughts as props or platforms from which to vault projectively other thoughts into the realm of the future, the possible, or a reconstructed past. I call this the *projection-to-project* or *double-projection* strategy. It is the essence of Imagining. The question, then—the central one of this inquiry—is what makes this strategy possible and why.

The possible answer I propose is *mental rehearsals*, of a certain sort, or what I called earlier *metamental*. It is the sort enabled by a cluster of abilities for double projection—among them the I-abilities of chapter 1.1—which evolved over many generations of modern human ontogenies for reasons (i.e., under pressures or challenges) and from mental resources specific to those ontogenies. It turns out that two versions of metamental rehearsal by double projection—hence two versions of mindvaulting, according to my metaphor—develop at distinct stages of human ontogeny. One version of metamental rehearsal by double projection, in early childhood, is running pretend play, and the other, from midchildhood on, is running Imagining.

If metamental rehearsals are at the operational heart of pretending and Imagining in childhood, then the evolutionary (specifically devo-evo) question to ask is what explains the rationale for metamental rehearsals—why they evolved, in response to what challenges, and how they evolved, from what sources and resources, and in what conditions. The next chapters aim to answer these questions. To anticipate my argument, both forms of mindvaulting develop for reasons or under pressures that can be broadly described as social—pretendful metamental rehearsal for mostly sociocultural reasons, and Imaginative metamental rehearsal for mostly sociopolitical reasons. Since both the reasons and resources for these versions of metamental rehearsals are vastly different, so are the resulting mental competencies.

3.1   Identity Crises

Imagination has historically dominated the philosophy and psychology of mindvaulting through a disconcerting variety of views. To bring some order, I will organize the discussion around several axes. Nothing exegetical is intended. The aim is merely to show that this variety reflects a performance or output level, leaving the more basic competence level open to fresh inquiries. For most of this section, until the competence for Imagining is carefully carved out and defined, I will revert to imagination talk with a small *i*.

Untidy diversity

Two axes along which imagination is conceived are its representational format and, relatedly, alleged primary function. Most people—philosophers and psychologists included—used to and many still think that imagination works mainly with mental images, particularly of the visual or pictorial sort. This is imagination as imagery or *imagistic imagination*. The mental activity involved may be described as *imaging*. Earlier and influential philosophers, especially in the empiricist tradition (John Locke, George Berkeley, and David Hume), thought that mental images, typically of the visual sort, were less pregnant and lively than actual percepts, yet more concrete and vivid than abstract thoughts. This is why it was thought that the function of mental images was to mediate between perception, on the one hand, and memory, judgment, and reason, on the other hand. This mediating role was viewed as passive and most often preestablished—you think of something, and an associated image pops up, somehow. This is "reproductive imagination," as Immanuel Kant called it.

Yet we know intuitively that in its imagistic form, imagination has more than a mediating role. It can also be active, constructive, inventive, or "productive," in Kant's terms. We can deliberately construct and manipulate mental images, not only of the pictorial kind, but of other kinds as well. From the developmental perspective taken later in this book, it is interesting to note that it is only after age five that children are able to construct and manipulate pictorial images deliberately and flexibly, even though their younger selves can do that well with action images in their pretend play. Young children may be reproductively imaginative in the pictorial mode, but they are productively imaginative in the action mode. To anticipate my argument, it all depends on what must be actively or productively rehearsed mentally, and which is the most appropriate and efficient representational format.

At the opposite, nonimagistic end, there is (what is frequently called) *propositional imagination*, which is capable of representing abstract, counterfactual, or even impossible facts and situations solely with conceptual and linguistic resources. It is also called *suppositional imagination*. This is the sort of imagination associated with the work of the intellect.

Intriguingly, past philosophers who used propositional imagination brilliantly to make their polemical and constructive points did not give it high marks as a mental competence. Plato thought that propositional imagining was mere supposing (*eikasia*), as opposed to genuine knowledge, and therefore dismissed it as an unworthy mental faculty. He did so notwithstanding the fact that this "mere supposing" stance was so effectively employed to reach what he thought was genuine knowledge.

With a more ambitious version of suppositional imagination, one can conceive of the infinite, world peace, various deities, Fermat's theorem, relativity, eternal life, even a noiseless world, or almost literally whatever. This is propositional imagination deployed *as conceivability*. It was made famous by René Descartes in his *Meditations*. Yet like Plato, after employing it so effectively to reach his Cogito, and thus the ultimate and only truth, Descartes dismissed such imagination as adventitious, eliminable, and unnecessary to true knowledge.

In general, a close look at the history of philosophical ideas about imagination reveals a deep ambivalence about its role and usefulness. For many philosophers across centuries, imagination has a lowly status in the mental architecture, particularly in its passively imagistic version, and yet in its conceivability or suppositional mode, it can reach high and far intellectually. It is only in the last two centuries, with Kant and the Romantics, that productive imagination got increasingly more respect, and its nonimagistic, suppositional version moved away from Platonic and Cartesian disrespect toward an influential center stage (Brann 1991; Casey 1973; McGinn 2004; Nichols 2006).

The philosophical ambivalence about imagination has had a distinct though comparable echo in developmental psychology. Two influential pioneers, Freud and Piaget, thought that imagination was a primitive, temporary, and maladapted form of mentation, mostly imagistic, that develops early in childhood, and was infused with wishful thinking, daydreaming, undisciplined departures from reality, and even hallucination. This is, literally, imagination *as fantasy*. Only gradually (they both thought) did children abandon or sideline fantasy, and turn to reality by way of an increasingly realistic and disciplined thinking. On the alternative and equally influential view of Lev Vygotsky, (older) children's early manifestation of imagination was productive, mentally consequential, and still active in adult mentation. As argued in the next chapters, the developmental story of imagination is rather complicated and different from these pioneering positions, but will largely be on Vygotsky's side. For the time being, there are other, more biologically grounded candidates that need to be identified and properly framed in the context of my inquiry.

The candidates examined so far were eminently cognitive. There is also a *noncognitive* side to imagining, as in empathizing, feeling somebody else's pain or excitement, or re-creating phenomenally a vivid experience one once had or could have had. This is close to the notion of "enactment imagination" proposed by Alvin Goldman (2006, 47). If spontaneous and involuntary, such enactive imaginings are likely to draw on memory along with various action- and feeling-mirroring capabilities. In that case, they will not be much different from unwilled, unbidden, and uncontrolled enactments, such as dreams—day or night—hallucinations, or sudden visions. As I read it, however, Goldman's concept envisages enactive imagination as an active, deliberate, effortful, and hence productive sort of imagination. If so, it is likely to draw on cognitive databases as well as abilities, resulting in a hybrid form of imagination.

So far I have sampled a variety of diverging expressions of imagination, or outputs of a still uncharted competence, as I will contend. Even if we set aside the unwilled, unbidden, and uncontrolled versions as failing my definition of mindvaulting, we are still left with little sense of what the productive, deliberate forms of imagining share, as a guide to the underlying competence. The picture is further complicated, particularly in the psychological and ethological literature, by alleged sightings of imaginings in abilities, mental activities, or minds that (in my view) do not really qualify. These I treat as false pretenders.

False pretenders

Since imagining necessarily goes beyond what the senses currently reveal, any mental representation or activity that fits the bill is in danger of passing for imagination of some sort or another. One such false pretender is predicting or expecting a future event. Many animal minds are capable of such predictions or expectations. Are they imaginative? Not likely and not plausibly.

Predicting or expecting an event need not imply imagining it. As I will note in section 4.1, the brain is a constant projector that anticipates states of the sensory inputs and possible actions. This is the brain's "default mode." The default projections as well as the projections caused or cued by sensory inputs tend to be reflex, unbidden, and unconscious—conditions that do not characterize imagination. Predicting in animal or human minds is of course projection plus, but the plus in question falls short of imagining, even in the weak, small-i sense envisaged in this section.

As they learn associations between specific kinds of stimuli and frequently encountered states of affairs, or make connections between such stimuli, action schemes, and ecological regularities known to range over frequently encountered states of affairs, animal minds can use such associations and connections to predict future states of affairs, usually by habit, and when cued by the right sensory or memory inputs. When it comes to hoarding food or anticipating shelter, hibernators do it, and so do many species of birds and rodents. Furthermore, dedicated behavioral capacities to register and act on ecological regularities, or alternatively, memory and learning, can also generate appropriate predictions or expectations.

The question is whether animal memory, learning, and behavioral capacities that exploit ecological regularities can lead to some sort of Imagination (the real thing, in a strong capital-*I* sense) under appropriate evolutionary pressures. I think the answer will likely be negative, in light of what is currently known about animal cognition (Buckner and Carroll 2007; Shettleworth 2010; Tomasello and Call 1997). Animal minds, moreover, are believed to live motivationally in the present, whereas Imagination is a device for extensive mental travel, as it were, with images, needs, feelings, motives, and ideas, or even distinct selves, often taken along for the ride. Being anchored in the motivational present as well as wired or habituated to expect few and specific kinds of future events are not conditions that suggest selection pressures for any sort of imagination.

Animal minds are also likely to be predominantly modular or functionally specialized, even when it comes to what is remembered and predicted, whereas Imagination is notoriously versatile and open-ended in what it can represent, and how. Modularity means domain specificity for cognitive resources, including memory and learning, whereas Imagination is domain inspecific. Modularity also means an overwhelmingly procedural and implicit, and hence cognitively impenetrable and unconscious, handling of information, whereas Imagination has explicitly represented images and thoughts generating other such images and thoughts in a mixed, fluid, cognitively penetrable and conscious mode.

If this admittedly rough and sketchy portrait of animal motivation and cognition is plausible, then it is fair to assume that
the abilities required for Imagination, whether imagistic, enactive, or propositional in format, are not in the evolutionary
cards for most animal minds. There may be exceptions in highly
socialized species, such as primates and cetaceans, and if documented empirically, the exceptions would support the position
taken in this book because of the intensely sociopolitical and
minimally cultural habitats in which they live.

In its productive mode, Imagination further requires executive abilities that are also unlikely to operate in animal minds
or even young human minds. Chapter 6 will focus on this topic.
One such ability is inhibition. It is needed to isolate what is
Imagined from what is currently cognized. Furthermore, to
deploy Imagined scenarios and infer from them, alongside what
is currently cognized, one also needs a capacious working
memory. Both inhibition and a capacious working memory are
not available to most animal minds, or for that matter, young
human minds.

At the conceptual level, a more insidious false pretender is
thinking—a notion even more promiscuous than that of imagination. Conjuring up a thought that is not reflecting or responding to a current input is often regarded as an act of Imagination.
It need not be. Imagining is a more deliberate, effortful, sus-
tained, and goal-directed mental activity than just producing or
entertaining thoughts. In general, the idea of thinking is so fluid
and elastic as to have no distinct grip on any specific mental
activity. It may simply suggest a mind at work behind the veil
of perception and immediacy of action. That does not say too
much. It could be just projection in the default mode noted
earlier or some sort of habitual prediction. Animals are said to

think, and so are very young children, but as I will describe later, whatever they do mentally is different and far from Imagining, as a capability for deliberate and effortful metamental rehearsal by double projection.

This admittedly rushed, sketchy, and unexegetical survey raises a legitimate question: Why does imagination generate such conceptual diversity and ambivalence in philosophy, deep theoretical differences in developmental psychology, and some false expectations in animal psychology? Why so many angles on imagination? Can imagination be, or do, so many different things? Is it one or many faculties? If one, why such disparate manifestations, and if many, what do they have in common, if anything? Why, in short, is imagination so divergently, often conflictingly, and even implausibly construed? Even though this inquiry is not a conceptual study of imagination or a deconstruction of its misconceptions, the next section inches toward an answer to these questions.

3.2   The Competence Angle

The views just canvased draw most of their inspiration about imagining from its intuitively accessible deployments or more reflective introspections of it. As a result, imagination is viewed from the angle of performance rather than competence. The intuitively accessible deployments of imagination and their introspection, no matter how grasped and analyzed, are *performance outputs* of an underlying competence.

It is a truism of cognitive science that a competence can rarely, if ever, be read merely from its outputs. For example, the competence for vision cannot be reconstructed from its outputs—the conscious visual images or their contents, that is, what is seen. The same is true of memory, grammar, and reasoning, among other mental competencies. Imagination is no different. Our intuitive or introspective sense of what and how we imagine, in either an imagistic, enactive, or propositionally suppositional mode, need not, and indeed does not, reveal what the competencies are (if more than one) and how they actually work. Nor can an intuitive or introspective sense explain why and how Imagination (or vision, memory, or grammar) evolved and develops.

The theory road

The path that the explanation of a mental competence should take is that of theory, not intuition, introspection, or conceptual analysis. Here I part company with many philosophers of imagination, but then this is not a philosophical book. Theory in cognitive science need not mean just psychology or neuroscience. It should mean, and will mean here, a coherent assortment of hypotheses and data in the relevant domains (biological, evolutionary, developmental, and neuropsychological), where the roots and resources of as well as reasons for Imagination as a competence can be found.

Before starting our journey on this theoretical road, I also note that the diverging views canvased earlier, while failing to engage the study of Imagination as a competence, do highlight some of its real properties or its use. Imagination does draw on mental projection, which is often used for anticipation and prediction; Imagination frequently does take the form of enacting mental states or imagery, or alternatively, propositional cognition or a mixture of the two; Imagination oftentimes does result in fantasy, idle daydreaming, or hallucination; and yes, Imagination can be passively exercised, when cued or stimulated by some unbidden input.

This variety of Imaginings makes sense from a competence angle. Any mental competence relies on more basic components and resources, and can have collateral or unprogrammed uses. Just as conscious perception depends on the more basic and unconscious vision, so Imagination relies on the more basic brain projection. Some mental competencies can operate with different representational media. Just as one can communicate with signals, words, and gestures, one can Imagine with images as well as propositional thoughts. And just as the exercise of the language competence can surprise us with unbidden or ungrammatical utterances, so can the Imagining brain flash unbidden hallucinations, dreams, and fantasies.

These observations are metaphysically grounded, if we care to dig deeper. Almost any disposition in nature (fragility, solubility, and so on) rests on deeper dispositions (say, moving molecules and atoms), and almost all dispositions are exercised fully when the right conditions are in place, and less fully or deviantly when some of the required conditions fail to materialize or are distorted. Mental competencies, such as those involved in Imagining, are (deep down) nothing but dispositions, and usually many interacting ones.

The larger picture
This last point invites another comment, this time on the false pretenders that were said a section ago to be viewed in some quarters of animal and child psychology as genuine Imaginative exploits available to animal or young human minds. The mistake in these views, I think, is not only to perceive a necessary condi-

tion of Imagining—namely, projection—as the real thing. The graver mistake, methodologically, is not to look at the larger picture and try to see whether the alleged competence for animal or infant Imagination fits plausibly into the wider matrix of other mental competencies and the resulting behaviors. Of what use is Imagination to a bird or rodent that uses it only to hide food for later—a probably modular, domain-specific, and hence narrow accomplishment, it seems to me—or an ape that takes some primitive tool-like stone or branch along the ride for a later, specific use in getting food and for nothing else? What sort of Imagination could that be?

If apes are to be credited with some Imagination, it should rather be in their sociopolitical domain of activity, where ape actions are incomparably more complex and versatile than in the physical domain (including primitive toolmaking or food gathering), and where, as a result, several other mental competencies are interactively involved, such as memories for specific individuals along with their behavioral patterns and anticipative computations over relations among several individuals (Byrne and Whiten 1988; Tomasello and Call 1997; Whiten 1991). Yet even there, I argue later, we may have an ape-typical precursor rather than the real competence found in human minds. And the same may be true of what operates first in young human children—namely, precursors. The difference, I conjecture, is that later developments in human minds turn precursors into genuine forms of Imagination—something that the minds of apes apparently fail to do.

How do we know all this? We don't. We conjecture. To gain plausibility, the conjectures should have a wide, integrative, and coherent scope. This is to say, the attribution of a mental competence like Imagination (or planning, reasoning counterfactually, or even consciousness) ought to reflect the larger picture of an overall plausible and coherent fit between the competence, its component resources and precursors, other competencies it services or interacts with, the behaviors reflecting the operation of the competence in question, and last but not least, the environmental conditions (physical, biological, social, and cultural) in which the competence is exercised, and which historically may have selected for it. I call this the *larger-picture view*.

This is a picture often neglected in psychological and philosophical analyses of mental competencies, where narrowly targeted and isolated intuitions, observations, or experiments are all too readily taken to reveal or deny the presence of a competence, particularly when the larger-picture view would advise differently. As this chapter intimates, the study of Imagination has sorely lacked the larger-picture view. (I found the same failure in the study of consciousness [Bogdan 2010, 2012].) The present inquiry will constructively and consistently adopt the larger-picture view, and also use it critically against inquiries that fail to entertain it.

What sort of competence?

So far, I have discussed the notion of mental competence in general terms. The only distinction I made was between a competence and its performance outputs. There is another distinction that needs to be noted: between what a mental competence is for, its function or job, and hence what it does (its tasks) to carry out the function, on the one hand, and how it does it, how it executes the tasks in question, or its operation, on the other hand. This distinction is now a solid and widely accepted acquisition of cognitive science, thanks chiefly to the pioneering work and methodological insights of Noam Chomsky in linguistics and David Marr in vision theory. This inquiry is *not* about how Imagination, pretending, or their precursors work—their neuropsychological modus operandi. It is about the functions of the competencies involved and the tasks carried out in exercising the functions.

The question, then, is how to approach the functions and tasks in question. Not all mental competencies are alike in revealing their functions. Vision and grammar are widely thought to be cognitive modules. Their domains are specific and rather well structured, and so is the information they handle, in a fairly self-contained or encapsulated manner. As a result, their basic tasks—mapping light inputs onto images of distal scenes and sound inputs onto representations of meanings, respectively—can (and have) become fairly transparent to insightful theorists, without the need to go outside those domains and modes of operation, and in particular without evolutionary considerations.

Such, I submit, is not the case with many higher-level mental faculties, such as reasoning, planning, pretending, and Imagining (see Bogdan 1994, 188–192; 1997, 49–52; see also the epilogue). Made of many components, constantly interacting with still others, developing out of precursors, being domain-inspecific, informationally open, and versatile in applications, the functions and thus tasks of these higher-level faculties are not easily transparent—at least not without exploring their origins and rationale. This is the spirit in which I approached intuitive psychology (Bogdan 1997), reflexive thinking or thinking about thoughts (Bogdan 2000), pretend play (in an earlier version; Bogdan 2005a), predicative thinking (Bogdan 2009), and consciousness (Bogdan 2010). This is also how I propose now to approach pretending and Imagining.

3.3   Metamental Rehearsals

What do pretending and Imagining do as mental competencies? What is the function they evolved to carry out? The answer I propose might look paradoxical, at least at this early stage of inquiry: as competencies, pretending and Imagining had not evolved *as such*, in response to their own specific selection pressures, which is why they do not have specific and dedicated functions in specific domains, nor as a result, their own modules, brain sites, and dedicated genetic bases. What actually evolved, as precursors and building blocks, is a cluster of capacities for *mental rehearsals of a certain sort*. As far as I can tell, and will argue, these capacities evolved only in human ontogeny, and initially for sociocultural and later sociopolitical reasons. The competencies for such specialized mental rehearsals, not for pretending and Imagining as such, are the outcomes of human developmental evolution.

Roughly speaking, mental rehearsal *in general* consists in anticipating or projecting as well as practicing mentally what could or will be done through some action, in some interaction with others, or in relating to an impending, future, or possible action or situation. The tiger about to attack from a favorite angle, the sprinter just about to take off from a favorite bodily position, or the carpenter looking for the best position to place the beam may all be mentally rehearsing, often unconsciously, their impending actions. Brains are designed to project and anticipate actions, most often by mental rehearsals (Bar 2007, 2011).

Mental rehearsals *about* or *factoring in mental states* is what people normally are very good at when pretending and Imagining. Being-very-good-at usually points to a core competence.

Relatively few people are very good at acting, art, or science, or even creative conversation; these are, as it were, extracurricular applications of the core competencies for mental rehearsals about mental states. The core competencies of (what will eventually underpin) pretending and Imagining evolved *initially* to do mental rehearsals by double projections of mental states, and that is why these competencies were selected and are universal in normal humans. Mindvaulting *begins* as conscious, deliberate, and effortful mental rehearsals by double projection of mental states—that is, by forming, say, thoughts from which further thoughts are projected. I call such specialized mental rehearsals *metamental rehearsals*.

But metamental rehearsals for what? My conjecture is that in early childhood, the metamental rehearsal capacity underpinning pretend play initially evolved to learn and master the sociocultural artifacts, practices, and norms of the adult world, while the metamental rehearsal capacity undergirding Imagining at first evolved to handle the sociopolitical (collaborative and competitive) peer and adult challenges of later childhood. I abbreviate the former function as *cultural learning* and the second as *strategizing*, and will explain them in chapters 5 and 7, respectively. It suffices to say now that neither cultural learning nor strategizing is a genuine pretending or Imagining, respectively. The former—or rather the metamental rehearsals involved—are the incubators and initial matrices out of which the latter develop, when other enabling and collateral abilities and resources come on board, and are used interactively, and when the domains of application widen and diversify much beyond the initial ones.

If these initial incubators and matrices are not yet pretending and Imagining, why would they—and how can they—develop into competencies for pretending and Imagining? What is it about those initial forms of metamental rehearsal that leads to the development of pretending and Imagining? My answer has two parts. The first is about thoughts employed as mental tools in metamental rehearsals, and the second concerns their employment in sociocultural and sociopolitical domains.

Thoughts as tools

I will phrase the first part of the answer in colloquial terms: when one mentally rehearses a possible decision, course of action to pursue, or attitude to take to a possible or future fact or situation, one deliberately and consciously forms thoughts from which one projects further thoughts in various sequences as well as combinations so as best to service one's goals. It turns out, according to section 4.1, that forming the initial thoughts is already a matter of mental projection, which is why further projections of thoughts from them can be regarded as a *double-projection* process. Double projection is the operational heart of metamental rehearsals of the mindvaulting sort.

At this point I want to insert as a premise in the unfolding argument Piaget's important insight noted earlier in section 2.2. It is the idea that the mental schemes and processes that cause tools to cause desired effects—cause–causation actions, as I called them—are those that drive the ontogenesis of intellectual capabilities. Metamental rehearsals, I now want to add, involve schemes and processes that intramentally—that is, within the mind and prior to action—operate with doubly projected thoughts as *mental tools* that are causally manipulated as the means to reach one's desired ends.

It is in the nature of tools to be improved, modified, linked to other tools, and used in new applications in new domains

for new purposes in a sort of "ratchet effect," as Michael Tomasello (1999) called and analyzed it. That would begin to explain
why and how, once in place and well mastered during ontogeny,
the basic competencies for metamental rehearsals engaged in
cultural learning, and later strategizing, can be reutilized and
refined for various acts of pretending and Imagining in a mind-
developing escalation leading to the intellect. This line of reasoning gains further support if it factors in the unique nature
of human ontogeny, sampled in section 2.3, that allows a non-
genetic, sociocultural retooling of mental acquisitions along
with the assembly of new mental tools out of initial ontogenetic
adaptations and solutions. This is the direction of the argument
of the book's second part.

  To get an intuitive sense of my proposal, I will illustrate
comparatively two kinds of metamental rehearsals with thoughts
handled as tool-like means to ends both in normal adult mentation and their initial formation in childhood. In a first example,
I (as an adult) am renting a car—one of those old badly designed
clunkers—and trying to figure out what does what on the dashboard. Tentatively, I anticipate that the button on the left must
be for the headlights, so I push it, but it turns out to activate
the windshield wipers. I do not have much luck with the other
buttons, either. (I should stick with Toyotas; at least their mal-
functioning accelerators and brakes are where they should be.)
What I am doing mentally (though not successfully) is rehearse
online (as I look at the dashboard and am about to move my
hands) relevant visual memories as well as familiar action
schemes by causally activating and playing with them in order
to cause actions leading to desired (but not quite achieved)
effects. Rehearsing online means (roughly) that the rehearsing
is prompted and conditioned by the current perception-action

context, and the projections involved are mostly perceptuomotor or imagomotor, and barely precede the actions they guide.

Fast-backward to early childhood: in their pretend play, I want to say, young children initiate and deploy pretty much the same mental moves of online rehearsing, when they bathe a toy as a replica of a parent bathing a child, or when imitating the mail carrier's behavior. So will I argue in chapter 5.

In a second example, I (an adult again) am talking to a friend and am about to reveal some delicate news. As we converse, I am preparing my delivery of the news and rehearsing how to phrase it. I am aware of my thoughts, as I rehearse them offline, not only as mental events in my head, but also as having a specific content (conveying information about some state of affairs), a specific form or structure, which I may play with linguistically before choosing the final version, and some implications, which I evaluate beforehand as possible effects they may have in my friend's understanding, state of mind, and resulting reactions.

I have the intuitive expertise to deal with these parameters (content, form, and implications), as does every competent adult communicator. The metamental rehearsals involved are entirely offline, often far removed from perception and action, and may result in no action at all. The intuitive expertise behind such offline metamental rehearsals enables me to anticipate these parameters and value them variably relative to my goals, the flow of communication (in this case), and my sense of context. This is to say that I can mentally cause these parameters to take desired values (specific information in a specific formulation with specific implications) in order to have my message cause some effect in my friend.

Back to childhood again, it is not clear when children begin to rehearse and handle their communicative (or other kinds of) thoughts as I just did, as an adult, in deliberate offline metamental rehearsals. But the first signs (I speculate in section 7.2) may partially emerge around age three to four in some children's fantasized conversations with imaginary companions, and then really take off in their offline strategizing after the four-to-five interval.

Construed in the sense just suggested, metamental rehearsals rely on *causal knowledge of thoughts as mental tools* in the service of one's goals. It is a sort of knowledge that only humans seem to possess and has major implications for mental evolution in general (Bogdan 2000, 42–56; 2010, 90–96). What can explain such rare knowledge and the metamental rehearsals based on it? In evolutionary terms, what could have selected for them? I thus come to the second part of my answer.

Minds in sociocultural and sociopolitical domains

Metamental rehearsal means a conscious, deliberate intramental preparation prior to and directed at some impending or future action, social reaction, communication, or further thought, when none of the latter can be easily handled in an automatic, routine, habitual, or instinctive manner. Metamental rehearsal, in other words, is needed and adaptive—and hence initially selected for—when means–ends strategies have to be "thought through" before being implemented in action, communication, or further thought. The question is what domains of animal/ human life would generate the strongest pressures for metamental rehearsals, so construed, particularly in the mind-formative periods of childhood.

My answer points to the sociocultural and sociopolitical domains where humans (but not most other animal species) spend most of their time and energy, and in particular where human children are most actively, intensely, and frequently engaged since birth. Why a sociocultural and sociopolitical ontogeny calls for metamental rehearsals in the first place, and why metamental rehearsal capabilities develop into pretending and Imagining, is what this book is all about.

It suffices to say now that children's metamental rehearsals in sociocultural and sociopolitical domains respond to at least three major kinds of challenges typical of these domains, and not found in any other domain. One is the frequent and wide-spread *novelty and variability* of the cultures, social institutions, norms, and practices in which children grow up. Consider an analogy with language. Children do not know which natural language will become their native language. Children's minds are prepared to assimilate language generally, but also need abilities to adjust this generic preparedness to the particulars of their native language. In addition to a general preparedness of children's minds for culture, social institutions, norms, and practices, metamental rehearsals provide the necessary *adjustments* to the relevant sociocultural and sociopolitical particulars that surround them.

The second major challenge is that children's understanding and mastery of the surrounding sociocultural and sociopolitical domains must necessarily factor in the *mental states and attitudes* of others, and (later) their own. Children interact and communicate with others, and assimilate adult culture by making sense of how the minds of others relate to them and the surrounding culture. Making sense of other minds, interpreting them, which is the job of their *intuitive psychology*, entails grasping, representing, tracking, interpreting, and reacting to the mental states and attitudes of other people. Those mental states and attitudes of others can, and often do, range widely over a variety of domains distinct from those immediately available to interpreting children, or have different perspectives on and interests in the domains shared with others. This domain transcendence and different perspectives challenge children to widen as well as deepen their mental horizons by figuring out in metamental rehearsal what other minds represent and attitudinize (want, believe, intend, emote about, and so on) in what terms, and with what implications.

The third major challenge is the *dynamic and fast-moving* reciprocal interactivity involved in human transactions—communication, joint plans and actions, conflicts, negotiations, and the like—which children again must figure out and master through metamental rehearsals that factor in the relevant mental states and actions along with their variable implications, especially in the early formative stages yet also afterward.

These are the main challenges that children handle *before* their minds become truly Imaginative. Their offline Imagination takes off when, to put it roughly, children move beyond the initial contexts of metamental rehearsal, in pretend play, imaginary companionship, and particularly strategizing, and become able to generalize across domains by treating their offline thoughts as mental tools that service their projected goals in Imagined domains that are distinct from those in which children happen to be cognitively and behaviorally embedded.

Having said that, it should be stressed that pretending and Imagining do more than metamental rehearsal, in their various, often innovative applications. This is because the abilities for metamental rehearsal normally engage different other resources, inputs, and databases, from action schemes to imagery, from language to memories. Since such engagements, as performances, can vary, it is no wonder that specific pretendings, but particularly Imaginings, appear so bewilderingly diverse.

3.4 The Structure of the Argument

For the remainder of this book, my argument will center on the kinds of metamental rehearsals—involved in cultural learning, possibly imagined companions, and surely strategizing—that (more than anything else) usher in, stimulate, and shape the competencies for pretending and Imagining. It is an argument about the ontogenetic possibility of these two competencies for mindvaulting created by the underlying metamental rehearsals in response to the unique sociocultural and sociopolitical challenges of modern human childhood. Those kinds of metamental rehearsals in turn become possible because the challenges in question force children's minds to recruit and orchestrate a cluster of mental abilities, which I call *foundations*, and which evolved at different phylogenetic and ontogenetic times for various reasons, most of them either unrelated to the reasons for metamental rehearsals or related to them but from different directions, with different outcomes.

Schematically, the overall developmental argument can be articulated as follows:

sociocultural and sociopolitical pressures → metamental rehearsals for cultural learning, imagined companionship, and strategizing → that recruit and network a variety of available abilities (foundations), themselves evolved for a variety of reasons → and that later generalize over many other domains as composite competencies for pretending and Imagining

I divide the formative ontogeny of these two competencies into two general periods: early childhood, roughly from age two to around four or five, when pretending builds on metamental rehearsals for cultural learning and imaginary companionship, and after four to five, when Imagining takes off from metamental rehearsals for strategizing. Metamental rehearsals by double projection are thus the fulcrum that turns foundational abilities into competencies for pretending and Imagining.

II DEVELOPMENTAL ANSWERS

Before Four: Playing with Culture

Pretend play results mainly from online metamental rehearsals practiced by young children, roughly between ages two and four, in the service of their sociocultural assimilation and conformity. These metamental rehearsals consist of anticipating and reenacting playfully various adult activities involving mostly cultural artifacts and practices, such as bathing a child, cleaning a room with a broom, eating with a spoon, or delivering mail.

These metamental rehearsals draw on and integrate some basic resources as their *foundations*. As mental abilities, these foundations evolved for their own reasons, having separately dedicated functions that are independent of (what I take to be) their joint contribution to the metamental rehearsals that shape young pretending. This is to say that these foundations evolved in environments and under pressures that individually have little, if anything, to do with pretending. Nevertheless, in response to the sociocultural challenges of early childhood, and in particular the assimilation of cultural artifacts, practices, and norms, these foundational abilities are recruited and integrated or assembled to enable as well as run appropriately adaptive metamental rehearsals of culture-driven activities.

4 Early Foundations

Four foundational abilities stand out as centrally implicated in children's metamental rehearsals underlying playful pretending. Two of them—projection and play—are evolutionarily old and shared by many animal species, whereas two others—intuitive psychology (in an early naive form) and (mostly perceptuomotor) imitation—are thought to be evolutionarily recent and most likely specific to humans. The former two abilities explain what is distantly and only potentially imaginative and playful about young pretending, whereas the latter two begin to explain what pretending is all about. The interplay of these foundational abilities designs young pretend play as a devo-evo response to powerful and persistent sociocultural pressures. The devo-evo design process will be the topic of chapter 5. The present chapter outlines the foundational abilities as basic stimuli for, shapers of, and contributors to this developmental process.

No attempt will be made to be exhaustive, nuanced, or exegetical about these early foundational abilities. Their study is a work in progress in neuropsychology as well as comparative and developmental psychology, involving different interpretations of the data, based on diverging hypotheses. This inquiry need not go into all that. A brief synopsis of the consensus on each

of the foundations should suffice for what is needed here—
namely, a succinct profile of the foundations and their contribution to the competence for pretending.

4.1 Projection

It all starts with projection. More than anything else, metamental rehearsal is projection, and so are, as a result, pretending and
Imagining. Metamental rehearsals and a fortiori pretending and
Imagining are of course much more than projection; they are
projection plus (plus a lot, actually). But all of them would be
impossible without projection. To play with functional metaphors, just as metamental rehearsal is the operational core of
pretending and Imagining, so is projection the operational core
of metamental rehearsals. I propose to take a closer look at
projection by charting a few key steps that upgrade basic projections to metamental rehearsals—specifically, feedforward copies,
internal models of complex actions, prior intentions to activate
such models, and finally, intended projections from models
(mere simulations) without action execution. All these forms of
projection emanate from a basic propensity of the brain and
take specific forms relative to what organisms can do, with what
resources and for what goals.

The intrinsically projective brain
The brain is constantly projecting. It cannot help but project;
this is its default mode. This is a fairly recent discovery. It was
initially thought that this default mode was that of spontaneous
conscious activity, reflected in daydreaming and hallucinations
as well as focused mentation, but then it was observed that the
default-mode projection is present even under general anesthe-

sia. It is an intrinsic and general condition of the always-active brain. This observation squares with the estimate that 60 to 80 percent of the brain's energy budget is used to support communication among neurons, which is a functional activity, or a way of doing something. The additional energy spent on momentary demands of the environment may be as little as 0.5 to 1 percent of the total energy budget (Raichle and Snyder 2007).

Why? What explains this febrile nonstop activity? What is its point? It is too early to tell, but the view gaining increasingly wide acceptance among neuropsychologists is that this proactive projectivity is for anticipation and prediction—of actions, possibly experiences, and states of the environment and their impact on the organism (Bar 2011). Even unconscious and spontaneous problem-solving, sleep-on-it sort of thinking or inspiration as well as conscious idle thinking and dreaming, day or night, are now attributed to this permanent brain activity of projection.

The intrinsic and constant projectivity of the brain is beginning to reshape the understanding of *memory* as well. Instead of being primarily a repository of information about the past, memory is increasingly seen in neuropsychology as a database for predicting the future and a forward-looking facilitator of responses to stimuli (Bar 2007, 2009). Memory is for the future, not the past, as a slogan may have it. This means that what is deposited in memory is primarily material for projections about the future. Instead of generalizing from past experience, learning itself may be seen as proceeding from projections adjusted to incoming experiences. Indeed, one model of projective learning gaining currency is Bayesian in spirit: beginning with a set of advanced predictions that form a sort of prior "mindset," the brain then generates best guesses about the environment, to be revised in light of further experience (Raichle and Snyder 2007; Bar 2009).

With this intrinsic and constant brain projectivity in the background, let me briefly survey the kinds of projections that may have had a bearing on the evolution of the metamental rehearsals running pretendings and Imaginings.

The bottom level: Feedforward copies

Projection has deep biological roots, for good reasons. Mobile organisms that initiate actions—adding up to most of the animal world—need to handle two vital cognitive tasks: one is to differentiate themselves and what happens inside them from the outside world and what happens there, and therefore to determine whether an information state or action is caused by them or the outside world. The other task is to monitor and regulate their informational and behavioral interactions with the world. I call the first the *self-determination task* and the second the *self-guidance task*. Both tasks require projection.

To illustrate the self-determination task, let us consider the classical example of the perception of movement. (Historically, this is how the neuropsychological notion of projection took off.) The movement of an object results in a movement in the image of the object on the retina. The brain perceives the latter as the actual movement of an object. When the eyes are moved voluntarily, there is also a movement in the image on the retina, which is not perceived as a movement of an external object. Why not? The classical answer, known since the 1950s as *efference copy*, *feedforward copy*, or *corollary discharge* (Sperry 1950; von Holst and Mittelstaedt 1950), is that in advance of movement, the brain makes a *copy* of its instructions to the eye muscles and stores it briefly in some sort of short-term memory. This copy corresponds to the expected or predicted effect of the eye movements. It is a *projection* of what may or will happen thanks to those self-initiated movements. The brain then compares the projection and the actual incoming information about the eye movements. If it finds no difference between the two, it "concludes" that its instructions were carried out successfully. But if the comparison shows a discrepancy between the projection and the input, or if the latter is absent, the brain concludes that either the instructions were not carried out, due to some effector malfunction, or else that the input originated at the sensory gates. In this latter case, if the movement on the retinal image has no counterpart in the projection, it will be perceived as the movement originating in the outside world.

Feedforward copies provide a sense of how vital self-determining projections are. On some accounts, feedforward copies are reutilized in new forms of projections in new domains. These new forms are richer in content and closer to being involved in the metamental rehearsals of interest for my inquiry.

Internal models

Consider now the second, self-guidance task. It is also vital for all mobile organisms to initiate and monitor actions that are successful in reaching their goals. Since even the simplest goals have some complexity (e.g., objects to be recognized, grabbed, moved around, etc.) and can be reached only by a sequence of actions, mobile organisms are under pressure to evolve *internal models* or schemes of their actions-to-goals along with the effects (affordances) of such actions on the world and the organisms themselves. Research in neuropsychology as well as systems engineering and robotics (and what used to be called cybernetics decades ago) has determined that control of complex actions directed at complex goals requires a more rapid and more effective strategy than feedback from the peripheral input gates. This strategy involves internal models with a *forward* estimative anticipation or projection of the desired state of the organism, the world, or both, *ahead* of the actions initiated to reach that state. Internal models thus become projected as *forward models* (Grush 2004; Jeannerod 2006, chapter 2).

In most mobile organisms, such forward models take the form of instinctive or learned action schemes as well as acquired expectations linking motor and goal representations (Hesslow 2002; de Vignemont and Fourneret 2004). The activation and projection of such models by motor intentions is most often speedy (less than one second), automatic, unintended, and unconscious, even when (on separate mental routes) the perception of the goal is conscious. Motor intentions are what John Searle (1983) called "intentions in action." They either implement more complex prior intentions and/or govern simple actions. Motor intentions usually lack conceptual content and are tightly glued to the actions themselves (Jeannerod 2006; Searle 1983).

Prior intentions

What about the intentions to act that are formed ahead of not only actions but also the motor intentions implementing and guiding the actions—the "prior intentions" in Searle's account? They draw on internal models that are conceptual, are formed deliberately and consciously, and normally project (through the concepts involved) complex goals that can be reached gradually by sequences of component actions directed at a sequence of intermediate goals.

These conceptual models of actions-to-goals, activated and manipulated prior to actions, operate particularly in tool use, pantomime, gestural language, and imitation. Both in the history of our species and childhood, these are the activities most likely to call for metamental rehearsals in a pretend mode. Significantly, it is in these complex motor activities that the deficit known as *apraxia* is manifested. Even though apraxic patients can perform simple actions, such as grasping an object, they fail to sequence more complex actions involved in tool use, imitation, or pantomime because of damage to the brain sites hosting internal models that project such actions. It will be relevant to the later part of my inquiry that the same apraxic patients are impaired in Imagining similarly complex actions as well as recognizing them when performed by other people (Jeannerod 2006, 12–16).

The last port of call in our journey along this projection route from basic biological anticipations to metamental rehearsals is that of the kind of prior intentions that anticipate projectively in some detail complex actions directed at some goal *without* executing the actions—doing it entirely offline. Prior intentions turn out to be key building blocks of metamental rehearsals running offline strategizing (but not playful pretending) and more generally Imagining, which is why details will have to await chapters 6 and 7.

4.2   Play

The next foundational ability is second only to projection in how deep and widespread it is in the animal world, and how consequential for mindvaulting. Drawing on projection, play brings on board skills, such as improvisation, online instinctive behavioral rehearsals, and quarantine of normal behavior, which all can be regarded as distant precursors of key aspects of mindvaulting. As important, play trains animal and human minds as well as behaviors for future routine practices. A distinctly human form of play—pretend play—evolved to handle the cultural practices and social routines of a behavioral sort that young children must assimilate, master, and reproduce.

Most mammalian species play, in the sense that they rehearse normal adult behaviors in somewhat abnormal ways. Their genome prompts them to exercise playfully and get stronger physically (an immediate benefit), and also anticipate and fine-tune the behavioral expertise they need as adults (a distant benefit). Significantly, playful animals do not confuse normal with playful behavior. They *decouple* their play from their normal goals and the contexts in which they are normally reached, *quarantine* the play in its own perceptuomotor envelope, and execute benign variations on (what would become) standard behavioral themes. Thus, dogs that gently bite each other decouple and quarantine their play-biting behavior from its normal goal (to bite hard and inflict pain) and normal contexts (aggression and defense). The decoupling and quarantining seem to be genetically induced, and the play approximates a behavioral norm in the canine world (Bjorklund and Pellegrini 2001, chapter 10; Smith 2010, chapters 3 and 4). Decoupling and quarantining projections, two crucial conditions of pretending and Imagining, may have their distant origins in animal play.

Animal play is also *schematic*, in that it reproduces only set action schemes that are instinctual and hence genetically programmed. The main selected-for job of animal play seems to be that of integrating perceptuomotor processes that are not based on associative learning or mimicking, yet are vital and species wide (Mitchell 2006). Human children are inveterate players as well, for some of the same reasons, often social, that many animal species are. Other reasons, though, that matter to my argument are specifically sociocultural and to that extent distinctly human. I quote a succinct account from a developmental study that surveys a large body of research and data:

Child play changes dramatically during the first 2 years of life, developing from exploration and functional manipulation of objects toward sophisticated acts of increasingly differentiated pretense. In the first year, play is predominantly characterized by sensorimotor manipulation; infant play appears designed to extract information about objects, what objects do, what perceivable qualities objects have, and what immediate effects objects can produce. This form of play is commonly referred to as *exploratory* because children's play activities are tied to the tangible properties of objects. In the second year, children's play actions take a nonliteral quality: The goal of play now appears to be symbolic and representational. Play is increasingly generative, as children enact activities performed by self, others, and objects in simple representational scenarios, *pretending* to drink from empty teacups, to talk on toy telephones, and the like. Symbolic play is a forum in which children may advance on their cognitions about people, objects and actions, and construct increasingly sophisticated representations of the world and relations between symbols and their external reference. (Bornstein 2006, 102; emphasis added)

Many animal species engage in exploration and object manipulation, sometimes playfully (Smith 2010). As the above quote makes clear, young children are interested in and explore how other people behave (mostly in sociocultural practices), what they do with sundry objects (mostly cultural artifacts), and what those objects can do, with what effects. In this sense, their exploration and pretend play look like ontogenetic predispositions to, if not preadaptations for, sociocultural tasks. Animal exploration is not functional in this sense. When it is, mostly among human-reared apes, it seems to be driven primarily and most strongly by the sociocultural novelties to which these apes are constantly exposed, as noted in section 2.2. It is not easy to distinguish between exploration, object manipulation, and pretend play in human children (Perner 1991, 52; Tomasello and Call 1997, 70), let alone in captive apes. What should one say about the human-reared chimpanzees that play with dolls according to human scripts, such as bathing and feeding, or simulate activities, such as eating imaginary food (Cheney and Seyfarth 1990, 244–245; Tomasello and Call 1997, 68–70)? Or about the human-raised chimpanzee Vicky, who put her ear to the picture of a watch or was pulling an imaginary toy through the house by an imaginary string (Heyes 1951)? Are these behaviors in the same pretend-play league as those of young children playing with a toy as if it were a person, impersonating a police officer, or aping a grandmother cooking pierogi? Do these chimpanzees display exploration, object manipulation, or pretend play?

It is hard to tell. It may not be an all-or-nothing choice, which is just as well from an evolutionary standpoint. Human-reared apes may improvise mental solutions to various challenges that later became genetically assimilated in their human successors. What matters for the present argument is that exploration of function and pretend play emerge where as well as when ape and human players are constantly surrounded by and confronted with the sociocultural tasks of understanding, mastering, and reproducing some standard handling of cultural artifacts, roles, and practices. To use a knife or to bathe—both for the first time—one needs to observe another individual doing it first, and then figure out what is involved and how to reproduce it. It turns out that on both counts (figuring out and reproducing), there are major differences in the required mental equipment of apes and humans, and also between the mental equipment of both groups, on the one hand, and that of other animal players, on the other hand. As I will note in chapter 5, these differences go a long way toward explaining why pretend play is exclusively human, why exploration of function seems at best limited to human-reared apes, and why the rest of the animal players are mere players and object manipulators rather than pretenders. Many of these differences are grounded in another foundational ability on which pretend play draws. This is my next topic.

4.3 Naive Psychology

As anticipated in section 2.4, the ontogenesis of intuitive psychology begins in a first stage of early infancy on a bilateral note, and involves exchanges of looks, gestures, and vocalizations, which convey mostly affects and emotions. In the process, I noted, infants first develop a sense of the mental in others— the invariant mental states behind their various manifestations. This sense of the mental is likely to be injected and factored into the successor competence that is able to detect rather instinctively gaze, and its direction, simple desires and visually based beliefs, basic emotions, and attention. I call this successor competence that develops in a second stage of late infancy and early childhood *naive psychology*.

There are major debates in the psychological literature over how naive psychology works (as a naive theory, simulation, modular expertise, or a narrative social cognition), what it is capable of, and at what age. For the present purposes, I don't need to go into all that. What I find characteristic of naive psychology is the fact that it is mostly a *procedural* or know-how competence—actually a cluster of several abilities—to register, recognize, categorize, predict, evaluate, and respond primarily to the *overtly expressed* emotions, other mental states, and actions of (only) *other* people. This is to say that naive psychology is directed at other people's overt relations to visible and concrete targets in some shared context, is active mostly online and when externally stimulated, and is egocentric and driven by current motivation. This generic modus operandi will be shown to square with the mental coordinates of the meta-mental rehearsals involved in pretend play, as analyzed in the next chapter, but not with those involved in Imagining, as analyzed in chapter 7. Conversely, given the critical role that naive psychology plays in the ontogenesis and operation of pretend play, the fact that the latter operates online and procedurally, and is action bound and driven by current stimulation (among other features), suggests that so is the naive psychology at its core.

Imagination for intuitive psychology?

Contrary to the position taken here, according to which intuitive psychology is a prerequisite of and major contributor to mindvaulting, an influential view in philosophy and psychology argues for the opposite relation: that some form of imagination is involved in the exercise of intuitive psychology in general and its naive version in early childhood. It is known as the *simulation* view. There are two major views of simulation—one modest and lean (Gordon 1986), and another richer and more ambitious (Goldman 1993; 2006; P. Harris 2000). The former does not presuppose imagination, and takes simulation to be the unreflective use of one's own practical reasoning machinery predictively employing data about someone else's situation and actions. This perspective is not in conflict with the line taken here. The rich view is, as it takes the strong sense of Imagination (with capital *I*), a premise for intuitive psychology.

In evolutionary terms, the notion that some form of imagination underpins intuitive psychology is not persuasive. As will be mentioned in the next chapter, apes are not even in the pretending game, except possibly and partially for some homegrown ones, let alone in the Imagining game. Furthermore, the (widely acknowledged) cultural and technological underdevelopment of apes and even archaic humans does not hint at great Imaginative powers (Coolidge and Wynn 2009). Yet both these primate populations had (and have) a rather sophisticated social cognition and possibly some rudiments of intuitive psychology (Byrne and Whiten 1988; Tomasello and Call 1997; Whiten 1991).

Turning to human ontogeny, I think Imagination is problematic in the first few years of childhood, whether it applies to other minds or one's own. Young minds do not operate offline, and are unlikely to produce Imaginative thoughts and suppositionally explore their implications. Nor, lacking inhibition, do they fully quarantine their ongoing mental activities in order to handle only offline Imaginative tasks. Young children also do not really plan or reason in any full sense (Bjorklund 2005). Nor, finally, are young children fully aware—let alone introspectively aware—of their own thoughts (Flavell et al. 1995; see also Bogdan 2000, 2007, 2010).

Even a weak form of imaginative simulation, as pretending is often taken to be, does not fare much better in relation to intuitive psychology. Young children begin to play pretendingly around the age of two, yet by that time they have already displayed a good number of naive-psychological aptitudes, such as recognition of seeing and gaze, gaze following, recognition of intent, attention and basic emotions, and more.

A plausible case can be made that both in primate phylogeny and human ontogeny, social cognition and intuitive psychology, respectively, respond to more immediate and pressing challenges than do pretending and Imagining, and as a result evolve or develop earlier than the latter (Bogdan 1997, 2000, 2009, 2010). It will be the job of later chapters to convince the reader that the very possibility of pretending and Imagining actually owes a great deal to a developing intuitive psychology.

4.4 Imitation

Unlike simple play and perhaps curiosity-driven exploration, pretend play is not an organic reflex, nor is it triggered by another organism's play. Pretend play responds to some challenge that an organism strives to figure out, master, and reproduce. It involves observing, learning from, and reproducing something that other organisms do—something that, for some reason, is worth copying and reproducing. This brings imitation center stage.

Many animal species reproduce some specific behavior observed in conspecifics or other species. Young birds can reproduce the specific vocalizations of the adult birds they hear, apes can ape humans clapping their hands, and infants can stick their tongue out in response to an adult doing it. This is *mim-icking*—a form of behavioral reproduction that is limited to a specific form of behavior, and ignorant of the intent, goal, or implications of the mimicked behavior (Tomasello and Call 1997; Tomasello 1999). Pretend play requires more than mimicking as a reproduction strategy.

There is a good reason why human-reared apes engage in exploration of function when interacting with humans, and surrounded by cultural gadgets and practices. Exploration of function requires learning what one can do with an object by watching others do it and then reproducing the result. That, in turn, requires understanding how the behavior of others relates to the object in question along with its functions and affordances, and also requires being able to convert that understanding into a reproduction of that behavior. Chimpanzees in general have the sociocognitive and learning skills to handle exploratory tasks. They also have the sociocognitive skills to represent how others (conspecifics or humans) relate *behaviorally* to targets in the environment—when conspecifics gaze or gesture in some direction, for example. Moreover, chimpanzees have the skills to learn and reproduce the observable environmental effects of someone else's manipulation of an object. Tomasello has characterized this ability as *emulation learning* and distinguished it from *imitation*, which requires in addition understanding the intended means–ends directedness of the object-manipulating behavior (Tomasello and Call 1997, 308–310; Tomasello 1999, 28–33).

To imitate, one must separately understand the means (or behavioral strategies) from ends (or goals to be reached externally) and aim to reproduce the means-to-ends effort even by varying the means. To do that, one must be able to figure out the *intent* or desire (as goal in mind) that animates the means-to-ends enterprise, and that is the job of intuitive psychology, in its naive version for young children. Only imitation, so construed, enables young children (but not apes) to play flexibly and even innovatively with the means to achieve some goal. This is what exploration of function may presuppose, and what pretend play definitely requires.

Wild chimpanzees (and probably other nonhuman primates) can emulate but not imitate, which is why they are not explorers of functions of objects. In contrast, human-reared apes occasionally engage in explorations of functions, sometimes playfully, and hence the guess that their improvised explorations somehow engage some (but not all) of the mental resources required by imitation. Tomasello (1999, 35) speculates that by constantly interacting with humans who show them things, point to targets of mutual interest, and teach them various target-directed behaviors, human-reared apes engage in some rudimentary "socialization of attention." As I will discuss later, a much-stronger version of socialized attention, which is shared attention, is needed for imitation and pretend play. Shared attention is not in the repertoire of nonhuman primates, whether wild or human reared. This is why nonhuman primates and all other animal species cannot become full imitators and pretend players, let alone Imaginative thinkers and intellectuals.

4.5   Executive Readiness

Playful pretending and, to a considerably greater extent, Imagining require the exercise of several *executive* abilities, such as forming an intent, initiative in carrying it out, top-down (as opposed to mere stimulus-driven) attention, top-down control, monitoring, metacognition, multitasking (since the pretender and Imaginer must also handle current online perception and action), and availability and transfer of information across various modalities, stored databases, and action schemes. Some major differences between pretending and Imagining are caused by differences in such *executive readiness*, as I call it.

One overarching difference is the online versus offline exercise of executive abilities—with the former present in pretending, and the latter present in Imagining. This online–offline difference is also reflected, in my view, in the kind of *consciousness* attending pretending and Imagining. Pretending displays *extrovert* or world-directed consciousness, whereas Imagining additionally displays *introvert* or mind-directed consciousness. There is a good reason for this parallel: consciousness owes its existence to many of the same executive abilities as those required by pretending and Imagining. The executive abilities that underpin extrovert consciousness are also operative in pretending, whereas those underpinning introvert consciousness are operative in Imagining. I made this argument in detail elsewhere (Bogdan 2010).

Deeper in the order of explanation, I think there is something else that pretending, Imagining, and consciousness essentially share: their sociocultural and sociopolitical determination, mediated by intuitive psychology. The latter is children's vital avenue to adult minds and behaviors, which in turn is the only avenue to an understanding and mastery of the ways of adult society and culture. To do its job in the formative years of childhood, intuitive psychology recruits and integrates a cluster of executive abilities that install consciousness as a durable competence, while also sponsoring pretending and later Imagining (Bogdan 2010).

It is this essential involvement of intuitive psychology in the development of pretending, Imagining, and consciousness that explains why young pretending (like young consciousness) debuts in an extrovert or world-directed mode and is primarily geared to motor actions, and only later turns into introvert or mind-directed mode and is geared to one's own mental states as well. The explanation is that intuitive psychology itself transits in childhood from extrovert and directed only toward other minds, in the first four years, to introvert and directed toward one's own mind afterward.

Taking stock

My analysis so far finds young human minds in the possession of some key resources for pretending and, to a small and distant extent, Imagining. Regarded as foundational abilities, these resources evolved and developed for distinct reasons, at different phylogenetic and ontogenetic times, having distinct functions in distinct domains, unrelated to the later reasons, functions, and domains of pretending and (rather minimally) Imagining. The role of these early foundations in what will become pretend play can be schematically presented as follows:

• projection → a basis for metamental rehearsals

• play → improvisation of variations on standard behavioral themes

• imitation → registering and intently reproducing what others do, with a sense of the means–ends structure of what is imitated, and a sense of the intents or desires behind the means–ends strategies

• intuitive psychology → registering, making sense of, and reacting to the mental states of, actions of, and social interactions with others

• executive readiness → deliberately and consciously managing the exercise of other foundational abilities

The potential for playful pretending is almost present in these foundational abilities. The question is what else is needed to turn this potential into the mental and behavioral reality of pretend play. The next chapter proposes an answer.

5 Pretending

It is called pretend play by most researchers, fantasy play by some, and symbolic play by others. Many, if not most, researchers think that pretend play is actually the real ontogenetic debut of imagining and leads eventually to its highest form of (in my terms) intellect-running Imagination. The advocates of symbolic play (Piaget, most notably) think that pretend play is less or not at all about imagining (with either a small *i* or capital *I*) but rather about symbolization—that is, taking some artificial or feigned object or action to symbolize, represent, or stand for the real thing. Somewhat in line with this view, a (rather small) group of researchers sees pretend play as relying on metarepresentation, thereby reflecting the debut of a genuine and high-power intuitive psychology. Finally, still another group takes a deflationary view, and thinks that pretend play is actually about curiosity and playful exploration of sundry novelties, and not much more.

These positions will be properly referenced and discussed in due time. The point now is to signal a sharp disagreement over the nature and function of what must be explained—the phenomenon itself. As with animal mentation, we do not know what is going on in the minds of infants and even young children: they do not introspect, do not know their own minds, and cannot talk reliably about their mentation, as they are in the process of acquiring and mastering language, and indeed developing a mind. Only theory, based on observation and experiment, might settle the issues, yet the extant theories are so divergent in how they view pretend play.

I find this lack of consensus instructive, in that it sheds light on the multiple facets of pretend play. To some extent, pretend play is almost all of the above—pretending, symbolizing, and exploring, all done playfully—but *not essentially*. Its essence, determined by its primary function, is the playful assimilation, mastery, and reproduction of the surrounding socioculture. This is its adaptive function. So argues this chapter. It is in discharging *this* primary function that pretend play is also explorative, and displays a pretend and possibly symbolization stance, but not necessarily as that stance is analyzed by the theories evoked earlier.

Although not yet Imaginative, the crucial importance of pretend play in the ontogenesis of Imagination is that it is the first deliberate and conscious exercise of metamental rehearsal by double projection of mental states—one that young children engage in systematically and universally in response to the sociocultural challenges of early childhood. Why this is so, how such metamental rehearsals work in pretend play, and what exactly is rehearsed are the main topics of this chapter.

The devo-evo strategy outlined in section 1.4 recommends starting from the initial as well as primary contexts and periods of pretend play. They can point to the reasons for pretend play— why it develops in the first place, under what external challenges, and in tandem with what other acquisitions—and hence what initial mental tasks are likely to be carried out to meet the challenges. The tasks in turn illuminate the mental resources that pretend play is likely to draw on, from earlier foundational and other collateral abilities.

On the critical side, I will contend that a failure to identify the right reasons for pretend play in the right developmental contexts, at the right time, in the right sort of activities, leads many researchers to misconstrue the tasks of pretend play and hence the resources needed to execute the tasks, with the result that pretend play looks more Imaginative, more symbolic, and more metarepresentational than I think it actually is.

Despite some valiant attempts to find pretending in nonhuman primates and even other animal species (critically surveyed by several articles in Mitchell 2002), a rather wide consensus opts for homegrown chimpanzees as the most likely animal pretenders. The reasons, explored in section 5.1, provide important clues to the full emergence of pretending in human children. It the sociocultural environment of humans that best explains the alleged rudiments of pretend play in homegrown apes and its genuine version in young human children. So argues section 5.2. On this basis, section 5.3 outlines a hypothesis about what the initial metamental rehearsals do in young pretending: impersonate adult roles in sociocultural actions. The last two sections examine the limitations of pretending in relation to Imagining as well as the contributions of the former to the latter.

5.1 Cultural Challenges

Ordinary observation and professional inquiry concur that pretend play is eminently social and cultural. Young children are inveterate socializers and communicators practically since birth (Adamson 1995; Hobson 1993; Meltzoff and Moore 1977; Meltzoff and Gopnik 1993; Trevarthen 1993, 2011). What they do during their second year, when they start their playful pretending, is enlist their social and communicational skills to make sense of and assimilate the surrounding culture, broadly construed, as well as language.

It is a banal observation that culture scripts human lives along with most human thoughts, attitudes, and actions. Developmentally, I suggest that it is culture that unleashes children's pretending. Paul Harris (2000) provides a masterly investigation that documents the pervasive cultural contexts of pretend play. (In this early part of this chapter, I will draw mostly on his important book, *The Work of Imagination*.) The preeminent and causal role of culture in the development of pretend play is underscored by the fact that the latter is most frequently undertaken in three kinds of cultural activities: playing with new functional objects and artifacts (toys, games, cutlery, various devices, etc.), engaging in culturally shaped behavioral scripts (how to eat, how to wash oneself, how to talk on the phone, etc.), and performing culture-determined social or professional roles (parent versus child, educator versus pupil, doctor versus patient, driver, cook, etc.). Young children spend a good deal of time and mental energy figuring out in a pretend mode what objects and artifacts are for, how cultural scripts should be handled behaviorally, and what social and professional roles are, and how they should be played.

Children cannot do this figuring out unless they can understand and reproduce adult relations to as well as uses of cultural artifacts, practices, and norms; and children cannot do the latter unless they also grasp what adults intend and mean by cultural artifacts, practices, and norms. Children's social and communicational skills, guided by their intuitive psychology, constitute the only window to other, mostly adult minds and hence the surrounding culture.

So construed, pretend play can be said to be a *social* enterprise because it draws on observing and imitating others, and often, though not always, it involves either an adult or child as real or virtual partner or spectator. Pretend play is *cultural* because most of what adults do socially, most of the time, in relation to other adults and children, and what adults train children to do, takes place in the cultural contexts of artifacts, practices, and norms.

Pretend play in a sociocultural surround develops around age two, and a cooperative and explicitly shared pretend play emerges somewhat later. Even solitary pretend play is implicitly sociocultural, for it usually reenacts something children witnessed adults doing in the past. Children engaged in solitary pretend play may be tacitly socializing by mumbling to themselves, and imitating others mentally or vocally, as they proceed with a pretend reenactment. A child may also first see an adult exaggerate along some dimension of a behavioral script or role pattern, thus pretending, in order to check the child's understanding of and reaction to what is going on.

There is therefore a strong *correlation* between pretend play and its sociocultural contexts of manifestation. I want to move the explanation of this correlation to a deeper level, as close to causation as possible. When it comes to mental development, I construe the deeper level of causation in evolutionary terms specific to ontogeny, hence the next question.

Why play pretendingly?

Why pretend play, when exploratory play could conceivably suffice to enable children to assimilate and master the sociocultural novelties around them? Why the *pretend* stance, in other words? And why does online pretend play debut around eighteen months or so, and stay particularly intense for about two to three years, after which new forms of offline Imagination begin to take over (P. Harris 2000)? I think there is a connection between these two questions, but before attending to it, let me look briefly at some influential answers in the literature.

Many and perhaps most researchers think that pretend play is a psychological adaptation with a genetic basis, expressed universally in a time-determined fashion (Bornstein 2006; P. Harris 2000, 2006; Lillard 1993). If so, the question is what could have selected for this adaptation. Different answers have been proposed in the literature. For other researchers, pretend play appears as a source, training ground, and even early manifestation of metacognition and metarepresentation (Leslie 1988; Carruthers 1996), narrative discourse about nonactual situations (P. Harris 2000), or creativity as mental innovation and suppositional imagination (Carruthers 2002, 2005).

All these, of course, are sophisticated and uniquely human abilities that are exercised in later childhood and adulthood, and are central to Imagination itself. A deeper-probing answer, somewhat congenial to the line elaborated here later, suggests that pretend play is an ontogenetic adaptation that serves to anticipate, organize, and enlarge the mental and external domains of other developing abilities, such as the ones just cited—as a sort of incubator of such abilities (Cosmides and Tooby 2000).

I think all these answers identify likely and important developmental *effects* of pretend play. They may explain the basic function of the play component, which is to train for *future* normal activities in adulthood. But the answers fail to explain the *initial* reasons for exploratory and especially *pretend* play, and its pretend stance in particular. Both exploratory and pretend play enable young children to learn to handle new cultural artifacts and practices in terms of their manifest or inferred affordances. This is why the future-oriented function of exploratory and pretend play is bound to be derivative of as well as dependent on a *present*-oriented function. Except for the position of Leda Cosmides and John Tooby (2000), I find the other answers to be too future looking and finalistic, and therefore to miss the initial and dated functions of pretend play in early childhood.

So if pretend play is a dated outcome of early childhood, as I think it is, the next question is what specific and dated challenges, beginning around age two and petering out after about two to three years, would call for it? Furthermore, if it is to be play, why is it in a pretend and not just exploratory format? The first question first.

Sociocultural challenges

A number of studies of primate and child psychology stress the role of sociocultural activities in the pretend play of captive apes and young human children (P. Harris 2000; Tomasello 1999, Tomasello and Call 1997; for a general survey, see Mitchell 2002). Along this line, I want to make the stronger claim that the sociocultural regimentation of human children is *the* major selection force for the evolution of pretend play and eventually, with a crucial sociopolitical addition, Imagination itself.

Since human-reared apes share fragments of a sociocultural environment with human children and are thought by some researchers to come close to playing pretendingly (in addition to other novel behaviors), it would be instructive to make some comparisons. Some parallels are obvious. Both groups are composed of young primates that are literally in cultural captivity, in the sense that both are surrounded and challenged by an adult human culture, on which they are dependent for their well-being, if not survival, and to which they are relentlessly pressured to adapt. Both groups are intensely social, communicative, and ready to copy conspecific (and even interspecific) behavior, and therefore are appropriately, though differently, equipped for such tasks.

Furthermore, both human-reared apes and human children face two sorts of complementary pressures, even though vastly different in the nature of and impact on their later mental development. The first sort of pressure, which defines the framework of young-adult interaction, is the *helplessness and hence massive dependence* of young captive primates (apes and human children) on adult humans, with their language, conventional forms of communication, and the rest of the surrounding culture. Mastery of all these cultural forms is imperative for two reasons: to satisfy the adults, obsessively intent on enculturating the young captives, and get the adults to do what young captives want. Rehearsing playfully is an old (evolutionary) trick for self-training and can conceivably be recruited for the new job. But why *mentally* rehearse, and why play *pretendingly*?

The answer comes from the second sort of pressure on young children and perhaps occasionally human-reared apes. It concerns the *unpredictability and escalating novelties* in the sociocultural environments in which these young primates grow up. Most animal species count on fairly stable environments during their lifetimes, which is why their (mere) play evolved to deal with predictable variations. The environments of human children—and to some extent human-reared apes—

are not like that. (Nor are those of human adolescents and adults, for that matter; just think of what computers, the Internet, and cell phones are doing to young minds and behaviors in just one generation.) Animated by a restless and escalating culture, these environments are changeable, versatile, open-ended, and innovative, with many variations on the same or changing themes—in a word, environments that are largely unstable and unpredictable.

What, one may ask, is so problematic about cultural instability and novelty? Think of role play as a major form of pretend play—perhaps its core, as I suggest shortly—and the roles themselves as examples of novel cultural tasks for the young. Members of any species occupy biological roles, such as parent, sibling, relative, and so on. In highly politicized species, such as the primates, individuals also occupy political roles, indicating power, status, influence, alliances, and so forth. Such biological and political roles are normally perceived through physical clues, such as sex, age, size, and behavior, to which all primates are sensitive. What about such human roles like teacher, doctor, or police officer, with their many norms and behavioral scripts? The observable physical clues *fall short* of specifying the complex mental and behavioral texture of such roles, as do the partial and relatively few illustrations provided by explicit adult instruction. The same is true more generally of cultural artifacts, public norms, and scripts, and ritualized forms of behavior and communication. How are young children—and possibly some human-reared apes—going to figure out and assimilate such largely elusive cultural novelties?

Making sense of the affordances and functions of these novelties, as practiced and taught by human adults, is an indispensable first step, undertaken mostly with the help of children's intuitive psychology and imitation. Yet it is only one step. An equally tough challenge is that the sociocultural novelties are made of themes with countless variations: clothes, pillows, toys, and other cultural gadgets can be large or small, and of different materials, colors, shapes, textures, and densities; dolls can look human, animal, or surrealistic, and can vary along many dimensions and shapes; behavioral scripts and roles are even more versatile and looser than that; and so on.

Play can weaken or suspend the grip of reality, improvise variations, and in its exploratory format, physically check out some of their causal consequences. Yet play is limited to behavior, whereas most of the sociocultural challenges of early childhood call for understanding how something (role, practice, artifact, or norm) is handled and why. Moreover, neither mere nor exploratory play evolved to handle sociocultural themes with so many variations that have to be figured out and mastered in their own causal or functional terms, which is why neither can be instructive or adaptive in this respect. To handle sociocultural themes and their variations, human youngsters must combine play with rehearsing and trying out *mentally* what is theme and what is variation, or equivalently, what is normal, abnormal, or acceptably deviant. To do that, their rehearsals must be upgraded to *metamental* because and insofar as figuring out themes and their variations, normality and deviations from it, and so forth, requires envisaging what adults do and how they do it, and that requires grasping their mental relations to what is observed and imitated. This, as I will note presently, is where the *pretend* stance comes in, as an ability to improvise and metamentally rehearse sociocultural themes, of all sorts, along with their variations and affordances.

Summing up, so far

Pretend play is a dated adaptation in response to the pressures to assimilate, master, and reproduce sociocultural novelties. It is thus a playfully imitative exercise in cultural conformity. Its dominance in early childhood dovetails with the fact that "young children are 'imitation machines' in that their natural response to many situations is to do what those around them are doing, and indeed they are very limited in what they individually create for themselves in most situations" (Tomasello 1999, 52). So construed, pretend play promotes and facilitates *cultural conformity*—its primary function. Pretend play is creative or rather improvisational only because and to the extent that it fulfills this conformity function (Bogdan 2005a).

By familiarizing children with the surrounding culture, pretend play lays the premises for their later induction into the sociopolitical interactions of midchildhood and school years, as these interactions are suffused with cultural themes and variations. In this sense, pretend play is an indispensable staircase to the next floor, but dispensable once children get there, as is the case with many dated ontogenetic adaptations and solutions.

5.2   Views about Pretending

If the pressures on and hence rationale for pretend play are sociocultural, what must young minds do to handle these pressures? What, in other words, are the *tasks* that are mentally performed in pretend play? The reader is forewarned that it will take two longish sections to come to what I take to be a plausible answer. Matters are not helped by the fact that there is a disconcerting variety of divergent views on what the tasks of pretend play are (reminiscent of the divergent views on imagination, surveyed in section 3.1). The disagreement starts with the species capable of pretend play, which necessarily entails disagreement over what the minds involved do in order to play pretendingly, and when.

Who plays pretendingly, and when?

Some researchers see several animal species capable of pretend play, not only the usual suspects—nonhuman primates and dolphins—but also badgers and perhaps other animal candidates (Mitchell 2006). Others see pretend play as eminently human, with possible but sporadic displays in human-reared apes (Carruthers 2005; P. Harris 2000), and still others view it as exclusively human (Lillard 1994). In their thorough survey of primate cognition, Michael Tomasello and Josep Call (1997, 69–70) are prudently inclined not to attribute pretendingness to the play of apes or other species.

The disagreement over who pretends playfully in animal phylogeny overlaps significantly with and inevitably reflects the disagreement over the mental tasks involved. For if the tasks are deemed to be demanding, they are likely to exclude minds other than human. As I will describe shortly, the tasks of pretend play are indeed demanding enough to exclude almost all nonhuman minds, which should not be a surprise, given the sociocultural pressures to which these tasks respond.

The timing of the pretend play of young children is also relevant to establishing the tasks involved. Pretend play was said to debut around age two, and continue actively for about two to three years. It turns out that there are somewhat distinct stages of pretend play during this period, which I think mark differences in the tasks involved and hence the mental resources needed to carry them out.

Susan Engel (2005) distinguishes a first stage, between the ages of two and three, dominated by a scriptlike play that reenacts (mostly sociocultural) events in the real world, the world of *what-is*, as she phrases it. This is the simplest form of pretend play, the substitution play in which an object is used as if it were something else (usually the target of some imitation). It is an *as-if* form of play that explores reality—the idea persuasively argued by Paul Harris (2000). A more explicitly narrative play begins to emerge when children are in their third year. Around age four they begin to tell more complex stories that gradually replace play as a format for exploring fictive or *what-if* worlds. New Imaginative practices, as I argue in the next chapters, are just around the ontogenetic corner.

Having estimated who the pretend players are, and at what age, I can turn to what their minds have to do to engage in pretend play. I will briefly sample some of the most representative views and then indicate why I think they fail to tell a plausible story.

Views about the pretend stance

Since there is no disagreement over the biological ubiquity of play and its presence in pretend play, the real issue is the pretend part. What does it involve? A wide consensus is that pretending *in general* is an ability, exercised deliberately and consciously, to generate mentally, infer from, and act on imaginary projections known to be inaccurate or different from reality (Carruthers 2002, 2005; P. Harris 2000; Lillard 1994; Mitchell 2006; Perner 1991). Aside from this guiding idea, there is wide disagreement over what specifically goes into each of the components of the ability to pretend.

Some authors see the pretend stance as *symbolic*, in the sense that the substituted object (or action) is taken to stand for or represents the real one—as, for example, a banana stands for or represents a telephone. Piaget (1945/1962) is the major proponent of the symbolic view (see also Bornstein 2006; Hobson 1993; Tomasello 1999; others use the term *symbolic*, but not necessarily the full Piagetian concept).

Alan Leslie takes a further and bolder step in this general direction, finding *metarepresentation* to be a prerequisite of pretend play. Leslie (1988, 29) also introduces an additional twist by insisting in his analysis that "when the child acquires the ability to pretend herself she simultaneously acquires the ability to understand pretense in others. . . . [I]f pretense depends upon metarepresentation, then exactly the same mechanism will account for both the ability to pretend oneself and the ability to understand pretense in others." Despite the generic use of the term *pretense*, this equation is meant by Leslie to apply first to pretend play. It has enabled Leslie and other experimenters to check—and misinterpret, I think—young children's comprehension of pretend play in others as a test of what goes on in children's own *production* of pretend play. It is only the latter that ultimately matters; comprehension matters only if and when it can be shown to affect production itself.

In his thorough exploration of pretend play, Harris (2000, chapter 2) posits four specific tasks: a make-believe stipulation that fixes the abnormal identity of an object or action (e.g., banana as telephone); the suspension of truth; the insertion of the pretend item into an imagined causal sequence; and a narrative unfolding, which unpacks imagistically or inferentially the causal consequences of the initial stipulation. There are other views as well, but as far as I can see, they do not appear to depart too much from the ones just surveyed. Each of these prominent stances faces criticisms. I will voice mine with an eye toward an alternative, rather minimalist, frugal, and deflationary account, which I will develop in the next section. Consider first the Piagetian idea of the symbolic character of pretend play. It is attractive intuitively (substitute objects assumed to symbolize the real ones), and benefits from the age proximity to word acquisition and young children's growing ability to report mental states as target related or intentional. These developments do depend on a grasp of the referential or symbolic relatedness of mental states and words, and also a grasp of the referential intent with which mental states and words are used. The question is whether the use of substitute objects and actions in pretend play requires the same grasp of reference and referential intent. As noted later, the pretend game is played according to quite different rules. Furthermore, the symbolization proposal has not survived experimental and conceptual scrutiny, particularly in the subjective and egocentric version advocated by Piaget (DeLoache 1995; Leslie 1988; Perner 1991, 56–59).

Leslie's metarepresentational take on pretend play has also met serious—and to my mind effective—criticisms (Lillard 1993; Perner 1991, 59–65). Children begin to play pretendingly around age two, yet on most accounts, they start to understand metarepresentation only after four. Also, Leslie's notion that the same tasks are involved in—and the same mechanisms underpin—the production and comprehension of pretending is rather implausible, particularly at an early age; the self-other parity in metarepresentation develops only after four (Doherty 2009; Perner

1991; see also Bogdan 2010), which again is too late for explaining pretend play. What is nevertheless true is that pretend play begins as and is eminently a social affair, either through imitation or exercised jointly, and therefore pretend-playing children are aware of and clearly enjoy the partners doing the same. But that meeting of pretending minds need not imply a similarity of tasks or underlying mechanisms.

The next target for deflationary criticism is the notion that pretend play requires an explicit and inevitably metarepresentational stance of supposition or even make-believe (Carruthers 2002, 2005, chapter 5; P. Harris 2000, chapter 2). In cases of joint pretend play, Harris (2000, 10) also talks of a pretend stance introduced by "simple fiat or stipulation." One would assume that these theoretical terms—which I will contract to *supposition* and its cognates in what follows—are intended to signify that young pretend players do not take literally what they pretend and do as being real; they do not believe, for example, that the toyish teddy bear is a real bear, the wooden block is a bar of soap, and rubbing the teddy bear's back with the block is washing a real bear. This is a plausibly minimal sense of playful make-believe. The question is whether young children actually engage in *supposing* in a deliberate, explicit, and metarepresentational sense. I doubt it.

To begin with, it seems to me that many researchers take pretend play to be a sort of offline Imaginative pretense writ small, and thus are tempted to transfer and miniaturize the proper sense of supposing from the latter (where it is operative) to the former. Both moves are unwarranted, as argued throughout this chapter. The gist of the argument is that the reasons for the pretend stance, the tasks it involves, and most likely the abilities that execute the tasks are different in pretend play from

Imagination, as are the different ages when these two quite different mental activities emerge and the different reasons for the activities.

To get more specific, play already decouples and quarantines playful from normal behavior, as noted in section 4.2. This decouple-and-quarantine maneuver should enable pretend-playing children to initiate as well as enter a separate perceptuomotor envelope with its own roles and action routines and improvisations, which are not confused with real ones. As consummate players, those children need not engage in an *additional* mental move of explicitly adopting a suppositional stance.

In its proper sense, the suppositional stance requires deliberately, introspectively, and explicitly opening a separate mental file for the pretend stance, with a metarepresentational sense of what one is doing, while at the same time managing one's current and real-world-bound perception, thinking, and behavior. This, in my view, is offline Imagination. I do not think children younger than four to five qualify as offline Imaginers, although they have already been inveterate pretend players for several years. Offline Imaginers inhabit an *intramental space* defined by a genuine suppositional stance, whereas online pretend players inhabit an essentially *action space* (inhabited by all mere players) defined by a distinct pretend stance of a perceptuomotor sort. I explain the perceptuomotor angle next and propose a different reading of the pretend stance.

5.3   The Action Angle

Unlike mere play, pretend play is more than instinctive behavior. It is deliberately initiated action, as exploratory play often is. Both exploratory and pretend play anticipate, rehearse, and reenact familiar or novel action sequences. Both exploratory and pretend play emerge and operate within action—and hence perceptuomotor—cognition. What is mentally done and what tasks are carried out in both kinds of play is therefore done from a perceptuomotor perspective. This perceptuomotor or—more simply said—action angle has important consequences for understanding the tasks of pretend play.

To begin with, the action angle makes the distinction between exploratory and pretend play less sharp or even observable, both in the case of human-reared apes and human infants, particularly when emulation or imitation of human adults is also involved (Lillard 1993; Tomasello and Call 1997, 69–70). Copying the adult behavior with some object and exploring what follows need not involve any special pretend stance, let alone a suppositional one.

As Katherine Nelson (1996, 100) observes, in playing with a doll, "the doll is a stand-in in the activity for the purpose of action itself, not for its object-quality or for its symbolism. The doll is useful to enact the play, but if the doll is not available, another will do, or some other object will be brought in. . . . It is the surrounding action—the event—that defines the role that the object is playing. The child's prior event representation enables the representation of the play object and the pretense action." I read Nelson's notion of event representation as being close to a cultural script or routine, and take that to be what the pretending children are trying to assimilate and reproduce. The object or action—doll, banana as telephone, washing something, and so on—are stimuli or triggers of cultural scripts and routines.

This action angle on cultural scripts and routines dovetails with two other key features of young human minds as well as those of apes: the automatic reproduction of action, and the inability to inhibit such automatisms. Young children are inveterate and almost cannot-help-doing-it "imitation machines"— while the apes are inveterate "emulation machines"—meaning that once stimulated by the right object, action, event, or memory thereof, they irresistibly enter that mode of action. In addition, these kinds of minds "cannot inhibit their sensory-motor schemes that activate whenever a manipulable object enters prehensile space" (Tomasello 1999, 131). These two limitations—automatic reaction and lack of inhibition—make it unlikely that the minds of young children and apes could deliberately generate a suppositional stance in their pretend play.

Putting things together, the basic idea is that prompted by the right stimuli young children (and possibly a few human-reared apes) activate perceptuomotor or action schemes of familiar or about-to-be-learned cultural scripts and routines, which often with amusement they execute behaviorally with playful variations. This exercise need and most likely does not *begin* with Imagining the pretend scenario (for example, the doll is a grandparent or the tomato is a football). The pretend item (doll or tomato) is just a substitute activator of the relevant action scheme, whereas the separate disposition to play allows exploration, and strengthens the grasp of the relevant script or routine. As Peter Carruthers (2005, 290–293) explains, pretend play takes off from action schemes rather than thoughtlike representations.

Based on this picture, there is nothing literally Imagined in advance in the minds of pretend players. Rather, as Nelson (1996, 100) puts it helpfully, those minds "project familiar activities onto simulated props." This is what dolls, bananas, tomatoes, and all the rest are seen as in children's minds (and possibly those of human-reared apes): simulated props. The perceptual or memory image of the prop activates the right concept of the real thing, which in turn triggers the action scheme of the right cultural script, routine, or event representation, and this scheme acts as an unreflective, spontaneous, procedural (or how-to), and hence implicit simulation that guides the pretend action.

Evolutionary continuity

The analysis just outlined keeps pretend play rather close to its exploratory precursor, as it should, because it makes evolutionary sense. Let me explain why.

The ability to engage in pretend play has all the marks (timing, universality, spontaneity, and function) of an adaptation. As so often in evolution, its selection is likely to have been frugal, incremental, by tinkering with the available resources. Exploratory play, already in the repertory of young children and other species as well, is close in exercise and function to pretend play. As already noted, some researchers even think that the difference between the two kinds of play is too small to be detected and may not amount to much anyway (Tomasello and Call 1997, 70). I think the difference is significant, but the similarities suggest that pretend play may have branched off its exploratory precursor, for the sociocultural reasons discussed earlier.

The incremental opportunism of evolution is particularly critical in the mental development of human children, in which extraordinary and consequential novelties—such as word acquisition, intuitive psychology, and Imagination—are initially and gradually installed as variations on themes, and hence in mental matrices, already familiar to children. This is what makes the installation of novel faculties not only possible but also so successful. If a mental novelty does not fit children's minds at a specific stage, it goes extinct. For example, word acquisition is likely to be initially viewed by two-year-old children as a variation on their prior and already-mastered shared attention triangulations with adults. This is why, in those initial stages, new words are likely to be treated and used by children as a novel form of directing attention to a target. The otherwise miraculous success of word acquisition piggybacks on the prior familiarity with attention manipulation (Bogdan 2009).

Something rather similar may happen with pretend play: young children perform it initially as variation on the basic and already familiar theme of exploratory play. The difference between the two forms of play, which is the pretend stance itself, lies in how young children metamentally rehearse and explore, in order to assimilate and reproduce, the cultural novelties they encounter. But what exactly does this pretend stance—and thus evolutionary novelty of pretending—consist of? This is the question examined next.

5.4 Role Impersonation in Sociocultural Action

Two claims have been entered so far about the pretend stance: that it responds to the ever expanding sociocultural themes and their variations, which force young minds to combine play with figuring out what is normal, abnormal, or acceptably deviant; and that it can be managed frugally, without suppositional and hence Imaginative commitments, from the perceptuomotor angle of action schemes targeted at cultural artifacts, practices, and norms. But I have not yet shown what the pretend stance actually does. What are young children actually pretending? The tasks involved in pretend play depend on the answer to this question.

My hypothesis is that the pretend stance in pretend play is (essentially though not exclusively) that of *role-impersonation-in-sociocultural-action*. Such role impersonation is children's main avenue to cultural learning. By itself, observation of behavior is not enough; playful reenactment as agent is what seems to do the trick. The parenthetical qualifier is meant to suggest that role impersonation in sociocultural action is the proper and primary function of the pretend stance, its initial raison d'être, although (like any competence), once in place, it can be applied without some of the initial parameters, such as role, impersonation, or sociocultural action.

This hypothesis holds that young pretending amounts to adopting a role to be mentally and behaviorally reenacted in a specific kind of sociocultural action or practice. The child bathing a teddy bear actually impersonates an adult bathing a child; the child talking into a banana actually impersonates an adult phoning and talking to somebody; and so forth. The adult need not be somebody in particular; it is the generic or prototypical adult who counts. Role impersonation in a specific kind of action or practice may be the first and most revolutionary departure from young children's prior predisposition for exploratory play.

Role impersonation in sociocultural action belongs to the first stage, and thus the earliest and most basic form of pretend play. This is the form that creatively, yet within the tight envelope of scriptlike structures, metamentally rehearses and thereby explores the world of what-is, which in my analysis is the world of sociocultural practices, artifacts, and norms, as visibly displayed in adult behavior, and imitated by young pretend players through their grasp of adult mental states in relation to what is observed or imitated.

Why role impersonation in action?

It is an obvious, well-documented fact that children's enculturation develops out of observing, interacting with, and imitating
adults. As mentioned earlier, children *cannot* help but imitate
adults (they are imitation machines), and once stimulated,
cannot inhibit the action schemes inspired by the adult behaviors, especially in novel sociocultural contexts. In this sense, role
impersonation in sociocultural action is almost a mental reflex
running young children's pretend play.

The adults doing new—and in children's eyes, weird—things
is what children first notice, and then metamentally rehearse
and explore on their own. That adults occupy directly or vicari-
ously the center stage of young children's experience, attention,
and feeling in the first few years of life needs no further argument and evidence. Decades of research have conclusively
shown that, and how, the bilateral child–adult and then trilateral child–world–adult interactions guide as well as structure
the development of young minds, from intersubjective communication to intuitive psychology, language acquisition, and
predicative thinking, among other central abilities (Adamson
1995; Bjorklund 2005; Bogdan 2000, 2009; Bruner 1983, 1990;
P. Harris 2000; Hobson 1993; Nelson 1996, 2007; Rogoff 1990;
Tomasello 1999; Trevarthen 1993, 2011). Through and because
of enculturation, the same is true of young pretending: it is
centered on adults along with their roles and sociocultural
actions, to be metamentally rehearsed, explored, understood,
mastered, and reproduced.

Young children's exploration of cultural artifacts and sociocultural practices and norms is predominantly imitative. Imitation requires not only a grasp of the intent behind a means–ends
action but also an ability to see the means as separate from

and variable relative to both intents and ends. So construed, imitation was said earlier (section 4.4) not to be present in the mental repertory of apes or other animal species, and not in that of human infants. This is why their play is at best exploratory. Imitation and, deeper down, the young intuitive psychology directed at adult minds make the pretend stance possible only around the age of two.

Since young children are inveterate imitators, in playfully rehearsing and exploring adult actions with cultural objects or sociocultural practices, they are likely to insert into their action schemes adult intents and means–ends strategies, and rehearse and play improvisationally with the means. This is what makes their rehearsals *metamental*. To be learnable and reproducible, those imitated intents and means–ends strategies must reflect, in children's minds, prototypical adults doing prototypical things in prototypical contexts. My parent bathes me, thinks the child, but so does my friend's parent; parents normally and generally bathe their children. It is such a role-in-action that the child bathing the teddy bear impersonates. Or think of a child playfully pretending to be a dentist, with a doll as patient. This is their role impersonation of a dentist in prototypically "dentisty" actions. The child begins by remembering and imitatively rehearsing some dentisty action schemes—the theme of the pretend play— while quarantining the current context of perception and behavior. The child reenacts the imitated action schemes on the toy, exploring with some variations the movements and bodily postures of a dentist—and likewise for so many other examples.

Prototypicality is the mother of learning, particularly in sociocultural contexts. It provides generality and normativity about an action or practice without depending on an exhaustive list of properties. Given the overwhelming prominence and authority of adults in the lives of young children, it would be surprising if the latter's imitative play and its pretend stance would not take in adult roles-in-action as a prototypical package.

Role impersonation by professional actors is a useful analogy for the notion proposed here. Actors inhabit a role, and (the best) manage to simulate the thinking, feeling, and doing defined by the role. It is not that the actor—or pretending child—*becomes* another person and abandons their real self. The job of role impersonation is to set aside the normal roles that the real self has along with the normal actions that the real self engages in so as to reenact other roles and their typical actions. The actor, of course, manages the setting aside and role impersonation for reasons, and with mental resources, that are vastly different from those of young pretenders. For the actor, role impersonation is a deliberate, disciplined, and highly trained exercise—a suppositional stance that becomes second nature, once on the stage. For young children, the setting aside is easily triggered, playful, and to that extent spontaneous; as noted, some perceptual or memory association, or adult prompting, usually suffices to trigger the impersonation. Once triggered, however, the impersonation in both actors and pretend-playing children dominate the role-simulation mode of their minds entirely: it is a pretend mode.

So construed, pretend play has the job of simulating, rehearsing, and exploring cultural artifacts as well as sociocultural practices and norms through the imitative impersonation of the relevant adult roles-in-action. Other species cannot do this, not only because they lack the cultural artifacts, norms, and practices to be rehearsed and explored in this way but also because they lack the required intuitive psychology to imitate others and metamentally reenact their roles-in-action. Deficient in intuitive psychology, many autistic children are poor pretend players (Hobson 1993; Baron-Cohen 1995). My take on pretend play suggests that the autistic handicap results in an inability to impersonate roles-in-sociocultural action and imitate from that impersonating stance.

Tasks and resources revisited

If the pretend stance is that of role impersonation in sociocultural action, what do young minds do in adopting it? What specific tasks are involved? For the purpose at hand, I will schematize the overall tasks of pretend play as follows:

pretend play = exploratory play from a pretend stance

pretend stance = role impersonation in sociocultural action

To handle role impersonation in sociocultural action, young minds carry out a suite of more specific tasks, most of them implicit in what was said so far in this section. Besides making these tasks explicit, we need to ask whether young minds are capable of managing them. The answer, fingering the relevant foundational and collateral capabilities, is in square brackets below.

exploratory play tasks

(a) generating new action schemes [projection]

(b) quarantine and suspension of normal action schemes [play]

(c) behavioral unfolding of the causal affordances of projected action schemes [exploratory play; teaching; emulation]

role impersonation in action

(d) imitation tasks [further parsed as follows below]

imitation tasks

(d1) grasp of imitatee's intent and goal

(d2) grasp of the imitatee's means-to-ends strategy

(d3) separate grasp of means, with the opportunity of envisaging alternative means in a cause–causation format through metamental rehearsal

Instead of a simple square-bracketed identification of the relevant abilities for imitation, a more detailed explanation is needed here. For my purposes, the imitation tasks can be reduced to two major components: emulation learning, and some intuitive psychology. Emulation learning was said earlier (in section 4.4) to copy and reproduce someone else's action and its observable environmental effects. Apes can do emulation and so can young human children. The latter can do better than that because of intuitive-psychological abilities that allow them to upgrade emulation to imitation and thus handle the tasks (d1) through (d3). The intuitive-psychological abilities involved in imitation were said to range from reading intents to recognizing the target-relatedness or intentionality of gaze and action to sharing attention about items of mutual interest. Once young children grasp the adult means–ends strategies in this intuitive-psychological matrix, their curiosity and exploratory playfulness push them to pursue the imitated themes through variations that metamentally rehearse as well as explore the causal affordances of what is imitated, and in so doing, enable children to learn and adjust their action schemes to the causal dispositions of the items imitated.

5.5 Limitations

This chapter has so far aimed to make a plausible case for the idea that young children have the reasons and resources to engage in pretend play, understood in a frugal, online, and perceptuomotor sense. Conversely, the limitations of the resources involved vindicate the frugal reading of young pretend play. These limitations speak against the likelihood that pretend play is symbolic, metarepresentational, and suppositional, and hence Imaginative—or almost so.

First of all, pretend play is *situated* and *action bound* in a perceptuomotor context defined by the child's current perception, motivation, and memory; the child's projection machinery is activated by some association of a stimulus with some existing action schema. Such situatedness and action connection prevent young pretending minds from going entirely offline, into the realm of pure thought, so to speak.

Second, due to its situatedness, pretend play is only *partially innovative*: it produces partial modifications in something that is perceived or recalled and mentally schematized as familiar or normal action or practice. Thus, a banana used as a telephone involves a physical object that is grabbed, placed near the mouth or ear, and listened or talked to, which is the normal behavioral script, but the object is different from normal telephones, which is a limited modification. The multiple mental models that young children deploy in pretend play are limited to alterations from a central model generated by what is currently seen or recalled (Perner 1991). Another way to put this point is that young pretend players are creative but not re-creative (Currie and Ravenscroft 2002). They can combine action schemes in novel, perhaps unprecedented ways to create situations partially different from reality (creativity), but cannot shift perspectives in order to represent and reason about things entirely from the perspective of what is Imagined (re-creativity). Imagination alone is re-creative.

Third, despite its playful and often original or improvised variations, pretend play is more or less a *reflex reaction* to something seen or remembered. It is no accident that young children lack inhibitory control, particularly of current perception and motivation, without which it is hard to open and maintain a separate mental space of Imagination. The latter, by contrast, can be deliberately and reflectively initiated and flexibly deployed as well as actively monitored and revised.

And fourth, the essential work of metamental rehearsal in pretend play is *procedural*, not representational. A perceptual or memory stimulus activates the simulation of an action schema and switches the mind to a playful mode, which in turn quarantines the normal context and causes a playful behavior. Representational contents are of course involved throughout the process, but they do not explicitly initiate and guide the process, as happens in Imagination.

Added to the evidence and arguments of earlier sections, these limitations speak against an Imaginative reading of pretend play. As construed in the next chapters, the metamental rehearsals involved in Imagination take off from prior, explicit, and offline thoughts that project as well as rehearse contents that can be entirely different from what is currently perceived or remembered, with full awareness that (a) what is Imagined inhabits the perspective of thoughts deliberately constructed for this purpose (suppositional stance), (b) those Imaginative thoughts are symbolic (represent something), and (c) in turn, they can be thought about (or metarepresented). If Imagination requires these parameters, as I think it does, then pretend play cannot be Imaginative.

Many researchers may be tempted to see the pretending stance of pretend play as a sort of Imagination writ small. I already made my case against this temptation. Still, as a sort of metatheoretical reflection, I would add that this temptation reflects an *essentialist* view according to which the human mind and perhaps some animal minds come equipped with faculties, such as Imagination, that are part of their nature or essence, and it just takes time and exposure to experience in order to activate, shape, and gradually bring them to full maturity. On this essentialist reading, pretending is Imagination at an early, perceptuomotor, concrete stage.

There are indeed some such "essential" faculties, as research in the last few decades has shown—among them so-called intuitive physics, intuitive biology, intuitive arithmetic, and early (naive) elements of intuitive psychology. These are thought to be innate and domain-specific dispositions with a likely history of natural selection. These essential dispositions do in fact mature gradually during childhood. Their maturation may be no different than that of other bodily organs, such as the heart, lungs, or liver.

There are, however, other complex faculties that do not fit this pattern. They are not maturing organs in the standard biological sense. Some such faculties seem to reuse more basic capacities, with initially specific functions and domains, in new ways and new domains, with new functions. Other complex faculties appear to be assembled during development out of simpler capacities, also initially specialized in their functions and domains. The assembly itself does not appear to be genetically directed, yet the resulting faculties are typical of human minds, since the assembly itself responds to typical challenges encountered during ontogeny. As far as I can tell, predicative thinking (Bogdan 2009), reflexive thinking (Bogdan 2000), and self-consciousness (Bogdan 2010) are among the candidates here. And so is Imagination, if the argument of this book is right.

Having separated pretending from Imagining—or rather how their underlying metamental rehearsals work—the interesting question is whether pretending nevertheless contributes anything important to the development of Imagining. I think the contributions are significant, but not in a direct and essentialist way, as explained next.

5.6 Contributions

If the essentialist view is wrong, and pretend play is not an earlier and simpler version of Imagination, why would it figure at all in the developmental argument about Imagination, here as in so many other writings? The main reason, as far as the present inquiry goes, is this: not being Imaginative does not mean not contributing to the development of Imagination. I see these contributions going in two directions. One is to create predispositions, either enhanced or newly developed by pretend play, that enable young minds to handle the new demands and opportunities of metamental rehearsals by double projection after the age of four. Put differently, older children may engage the new kinds of Imaginative metamental rehearsals with a readiness at least partly shaped by predispositions acquired during the earlier pretending phase. In the other direction, pretend play familiarizes children with the new sociocultural environment, allowing them later to focus on still newer socio-political challenges.

New predispositions

What follows is a matter of comparative speculation. It is comparative because it reflects a comparison between the tasks and basic coordinates of the metamental rehearsals that initially run cultural learning by role impersonation versus strategizing, which are the incubators of pretending and Imagining, respectively. It is speculative because I extrapolate from research and data originally dealing with other matters.

Sociocultural rehearsals

One key dimension of future Imaginative practices, to which young children are clearly sensitized by pretend play, is *metamentally rehearsing* sociocultural novelties in terms of typicality and variations. As I will discuss in chapter 7, the earliest offline metamental rehearsals for sociopolitical strategizing benefit mightily from this preparedness.

Means–ends distinction

Within the sociocultural rehearsal space of pretend play, there may also emerge an incipient sense of another major dimension of Imagination. It is a sense that there is a *means/ends distinction* in what one metamentally rehearses, in the sense that one can creatively rehearse the means while keeping the ends fixed. Young pretenders reproduce a given practice (say, washing somebody or talking on the phone) as a fixed goal while improvising variations in the means used. There is solid evidence that young children not only distinguish means from ends, when observing somebody engaged in a goal-directed activity, but also distinguish means that are accidentally versus intentionally employed to reach the goal (Meltzoff 1995; see also Carpenter, Akhtar, and Tomasello 1998). Pretend play is primarily about rehearsing through understanding, mastering, and reproducing the means intended by the adults who are imitated or impersonated. Imagination is also about metamentally and often playfully rehearsing offline means to some end.

Script narrativity

A third and critical dimension of future Imagination, antici-pated in pretend play, is a sort of simplistic and schematic *script narrativity*, as I call it. The imitative and intuitive-psychological aptitudes of young children predispose them in general to parse what they observe, and aim to understand and reproduce in sociocultural contexts into scripts, routines, situation models, and other typical events as well as situations (P. Harris 2000; Nelson 1986, 2007; Nicolopoulou 2006; Zwann 1999).

Script narrativity becomes an essential ingredient of child and adult mentation as a ready-made formula to parse the sur-rounding sociocultural reality. Script narrativity structures the development and deployment of social perception, memory, intuitive psychology, and reasoning (Bogdan 1997; P. Harris 2000; Nelson 1996). These are immensely important contribu-tions to mental developments in later childhood and the opera-tion of adult minds, including that of Imagination.

Some researchers regard pretend play as genuinely narrative, in the sense of being an enactment of narrative scenarios. Thus Vivian Paley (1990, 4) writes that "play . . . is story in action, just as storytelling is play put into narrative form." Other researchers see pretend play, and role play specifically, as con-tinuous with and rather similar to storytelling and the adult handling of narratives (P. Harris 2000, 48–54).

My take on the matter is somewhat different. I see script narrativity as a major contribution of pretend play to linguistic narrativity and explicit storytelling, but one that is independent of and prior to the latter. I agree with Ageliki Nicolopoulou (2006) that pretend play and hence (on my analysis) script nar-rativity develop independently of and in parallel with storytell-ing, and are integrated only gradually in the preschool years.

Unlike Paul Harris (2000), who sees pretending as Imaginative to begin with and the young intuitive psychology as Imaginative simulation, I do not think that in pretend play, role impersonation, and their understanding of stories, young children take the *mental* perspectives of others, for I do not think that children have the intuitive-psychological resources for that and in particular lack metarepresentation (as I will argue in chapters 6 and 7).

Young children can inhabit a script, and act according to it and its functional perspective, for this is precisely what pretend play enables them to do, but that is different from adopting the mental perspective of others or one's own in a possible situation. This difference would suggest (to me) that when young children listen to a story and understand its characters, they (the listening children) adopt the world and scripts in which the characters find themselves, but not their *mental* states.

Furthermore, the fact that in listening to and being absorbed in a story, the minds of young children go offline need not entail that their mindvaulting is Imaginative in the sense of later years. For one thing, the test of Imaginativeness, as I construe it, is in active production and metamental rehearsal especially, not in reproduction or comprehension, as already noted in chapter 3. The minds of young children surely go offline, dealing with facts not currently in front of their eyes, when remembering something semantically or episodically. This is reproductive memory, so to speak. But before the four-to-five interval, young children do not engage in the productive memory of the autobiographical sort, as discussed in sections 6.4 and 7.3. Only the latter would indicate Imaginative memory. Finally, in using language, young children surely describe things that are not currently in view, indicating an offline grasp of things. The point, however, is that the offline mode of memory or language use is relatively passive, and at best suggests powers of imagination (with a small *i*, according to section 3.1), but not active metamental rehearsals with double projection of mental states in a suppositional mode—the hallmark of Imagination.

To sum up, I see a distinction between pretend script narrativity (in early childhood) and Imaginative narrativity (after the age of four). The former develops out of young children's induction into the pretend-play re-creation of sociocultural scripts. It is the assimilation of these scripts that is the primary phenomenon. The script-narrative format of assimilation, due to the complexity and thematic continuity as well as sequencing of many sociocultural scripts, is an effect, hugely beneficial to later developments in linguistic narrativity, at least in my reading of the evidence (Engel 2005; Kavanaugh and Engel 1998). But taking the perspective of mental states in script narratives is not yet in the cognitive equipment of young pretend players.

The intentional envelope

For young minds, figuring out what cultural practices and social norms are, and what artifacts are for, is hard enough. Figuring all these out *through the minds of others* is harder still. This is what imitation and cultural learning by role impersonation are all about. Young children assimilate the sociocultural world around them by interacting with others in shared attention, joint actions, and games that introduce them to various sociocultural items, such as practices, artifacts, norms of social behavior, and words. To make sense of all these novelties, children must discern their intended function and use, and for that they need to discern the intents and other attitudes behind the observed behaviors of adults. In the process—and as a result—of doing all this discerning, young children come to regard cultural practices and artifacts, social norms as well as words and utterances, as having (what Tomasello calls) *intentional affordances*, reflecting (in children's minds) the mental and behavioral relations that adults have to those items.

Pretend play is creative and often improvisational with such intentional affordances decoupled from their original embodiment (Tomasello 1999, 84–85). The decoupling is still online and mostly perceptuomotor. It nevertheless indicates that in both actual cultural learning and pretend behavior, young minds operate in (what I call) an *intentional envelope* made out of the intentional affordances of sociocultural items, such as artifacts, practices, norms, words, and utterances. In the strategic metamental rehearsals that develop after age four to five, leading up to Imagination, the decoupling and grasp of intentional affordances move inside the mind, and are managed offline, from a suppositional and metarepresentational stance.

What I think is immensely important about children's grasp of the intentional affordances of (what may be called collectively) sociocultural items is that gradually it becomes second nature in thinking and communicating about as well as dealing with such items. The intentional envelope is internalized and mentalized, so to speak. Young children know what, say, forks are because they initially learn what forks are for (function), and they learn what forks are for because initially they see, understand, and imitate what adults do with forks. This latter accomplishment in turn is made possible by their intuitive psychology that enables children to detect the intents along with means–ends attitudes and behaviors that adults display toward forks.

This is the sense in which children's understanding of forks and countless other sociocultural items, linguistic ones included, is "intentionalized." Later in childhood, this understanding becomes "fossilized," routinized, and compiled, and most often freed of its early and explicit intentional connotations. Young children initially discern linguistic meaning, in a Gricean account read developmentally, in the intentional terms of adult mental states, before that meaning is fossilized and compiled in appropriate conceptual and imagistic structures (Bogdan 2009). Likewise, for young children in the pretend-play years, the intentionalized understanding of the surrounding socioculture is paramount.

As such, this intentionalized understanding of culture and social patterns contributes mightily to the development of children's Imaginative powers. For one thing, inferring the function of a sociocultural item from the attitudes and actions of adults is surely a mind stretcher. More important, though, I conjecture that the intentional envelope of pretend play and resulting intentionalized understanding of the surrounding socioculture will facilitate (in the "zone of proximal development" [ZPD, for short] sense outlined next) the later development of Imaginative metamental rehearsals.

Review from a ZPD perspective

I propose to look back at the argument of this chapter in terms of ZPD, an influential hypothesis made by Lev Vygotsky. What happens in a ZPD is that precursor or incipient abilities that are not yet fully matured organically, or alternatively, not fully developed from some prior ZPDs, are "hijacked" socioculturally, and retooled, upgraded, and assembled into new abilities, which themselves may become inputs to new ZPDs. The sociocultural hijacking not only takes the form of adult guidance and peer interaction but also, and crucially, includes obligatory cognitive

responses to new sociocultural challenges and tasks, as in
pretend play.

Although Vygotsky does not discuss pretend play in connection with ZPD (but looks at imagination and play in general in
another essay [Vygotsky 1935/1978]), he nevertheless comes
close to it by bringing imitation into the picture. With typical
prescient insight, he notes that

primates cannot be taught (in the human sense of the word) through
imitation, nor can their intellect be developed, because they have no
zone of proximal development. . . . Children can imitate a variety of
actions that go well beyond the limits of their own capabilities. Using
imitation, children are capable of doing much more in collective activity
or under the guidance of adults." (ibid., 88)

The "much more" in question is due to the fact that within
the ZPD of pretend play, exploration, imitation, and mainly role
impersonation in sociocultural action, mentioned earlier as the
principal activities involved in pretend play, "awaken a variety
of internal developmental processes that are able to operate only
when the child is interacting with people in his environment
and in cooperation with his peers. Once these processes are
internalized, they become part of the child's independent developmental achievement" (ibid., 90).

In the ZPD terms of early childhood, then, it can be said that
the foundational abilities for projection, play, imitation, and
intuitive psychology, among other contributing resources, operate as inputs in a developmental zone, where they are recruited,
retooled, upgraded, and assembled by the metamental rehearsals for cultural learning in response to specific and dated
sociocultural demands. The result is pretend play. The abilities
entering the ZPD of pretend play can be said to have been either
underdeveloped or developed for initially different functions,

before being converted by pretend play into new predispositions. The latter are specific contributions—some surveyed earlier, such as sociocultural rehearsals, script narrativity, and intentionalization—to the next developments in Imagination. These specific contributions in turn may be underdeveloped or have dedicated functions in pretend play and other activities of the same early period before being recruited, retooled, and upgraded by the next developments in new ZPDs after the age of four. The online sociocultural rehearsals and script narrativity of pretend play are clearly underdeveloped abilities when compared with the offline Imagination and narration that emerge in later childhood.

After Four: Others and Self

In his insightful analysis of pretending (already evoked in chapter 5), Carruthers (2005, 296) asks at some point, "Why does the child actually act, picking up the banana and pretending to dial? Why doesn't she keep the whole sequence in her head? Why is pretending better than imagining?" His answer is that imagining is "hard work" whereas playful pretending, by externalizing what is represented, enables the perception of one's actions to take up most of the mental load. Imagining is indeed hard work and playful pretending is much easier, in part because the latter works as Carruthers suggests.

Yet I think the deeper reason why young pretenders do not Imagine is that until around age four, they simply *cannot* Imagine (in the strong sense adopted here). Imagination for them is not just hard, it is nearly impossible. Young children lack the mental machinery for Imagination. And furthermore, given my analysis, they do not *have to* Imagine because they do not yet register and respond to the significantly new socio-political pressures that would call for the development and use of this new machinery. As a result, the older minds that Imagine offline are not only significantly different from the young minds that playfully pretend online but also unlikely to mature gradually their Imaginative resources out of the resources for pretend play.

The next two chapters elaborate and defend these propositions. Chapter 6 traces the development of key components of the new mental machinery of Imagining—its new foundations. Chapter 7 examines the sociopolitical pressures in response to which a new kind of mental activity, which I call *strategizing*, assembles these components into the initial matrix and incubator of Imagining. The reader is reminded that (as in the case of pretending) the aim here is not a full account of Imagining or how it works in detail. The narrower agenda, rather, is to demonstrate the predominantly sociopolitical reasons for Imagination, its origins in a mental activity (i.e., strategizing) spawned by these reasons, the role of this new mental activity in assembling the resources for Imagining, and the significant, if not radical, departure in the modus operandi of Imagination from early playful pretending.

6   Change of Mind

Unlike young pretend play, offline Imagining is intuitively accessible to adult minds. So to get started with a somewhat analytic profile of my explanandum, I will expand the earlier list of I-abilities from section 1.1 and rely on the reader's intuitions to recognize from inside what is going on in Imagining. I divide these abilities into executive (in italics) and cognitive (in capital letters), as follows:

executive abilities

To imagine offline, one must be able to

• consciously and deliberately *intend* to engage in offline imagining

• *project* what is imagined *offline*

• *inhibit* online mentation to the extent needed by the offline projections

• *quarantine* what is imagined from what is concurrently known to be real

• *actively search memory* for the right information to be used

• *combine* thoughts and other mental states *from several modalities* (perception, memory, communication, imagery, emotion, etc.)

• if what is imagined is complex, *hold in mind* (actually in working memory) a set of related thoughts that constitute or are relevant to what is imagined

• exercise *top-down attention* to and *intentful control* of one's offline thoughts involved

• monitor and regulate *metacognitively* what is being done with projective thoughts

cognitive abilities

To imagine offline, one must also be able to

• SUSPEND the truth-value and even modal (possibility, probability, etc.) as well as doxastic (or belief-relevant) status of what is imagined

• ADOPT THE PERSPECTIVE of an imaginative projection

• use what is imagined from the adopted perspective SUPPOSITIONALLY as a basis or premise for further imaginative projections and inferences

• DEPLOY such further projections and inferences in a THEMATICALLY CONNECTED manner

• have a METAREPRESENTATIONAL SENSE that one's own offline thoughts represent something imagined, including something imagined about one's projected self as well as its thoughts and attitudes

• MIX or CONNECT imagined contents ACROSS DOMAINS

The task of this chapter is to explain where most of these abilities come from, after the age of four. Section 6.1 samples the psychological literature for various signs that the minds of older children slowly turn offline and become increasingly able to handle tasks that anticipate those of Imagination. Section 6.2

turns to the dramatic though gradual revolution in executive readiness that enables older children to inhibit current mentation and shift their interest and focus to alternative mental frames, in which it becomes possible to envisage and explore offline nonactual worlds from alternative perspectives. This possibility becomes mental reality, according to section 6.3, when a new intuitive psychology, capable of metarepresentation, enables older children to switch their minds to alternative perspectives—initially only those of other minds—from where to contemplate facts and situations different from those of their own current mentation. According to section 6.4, to do its work in the new sociopolitical ecology impacting on the minds and actions of older children (and examined in chapter 7), the same intuitive psychology conspires with the new executive abilities to shift children's previously extrovert mentation toward their own thoughts, attitudes, and selves.

As emphasized on several occasions, the capacity to Imagine does not depend only on the abilities listed above and explored in this chapter. Many others are involved as enabling or collateral resources, from memory and inference to language. Furthermore, as in biological evolution, so in its mental version: many adaptations and other enablers must be in place, for a variety of reasons, before new mental capacities evolve in response to new challenges. It is anybody's guess what and how many prior adaptations and enablers must be in place around age four to five to create the conditions as well as provide the resources for the development and full operation of Imagining. The abilities examined below nevertheless define the very possibility of Imagination, or its core infrastructure, as we may think of it.

6.1   Increasingly Offline

Even before we get to the core infrastructure (in the next section), we can get a sense of how the minds of older children go increasingly offline after age four by sampling some of the other mental activities they become able to engage in and that will be involved in their Imaginings.

Mental imagery

There is no need to emphasize the immense role of mental imagery in Imagination. The offline construction and manipulation of mental images are deliberate mental acts, and thus reliable measures of the capacity to Imagine, as I construe it. Given their difficulties with mental rotation—a standard test for *productive* or constructive mental imagery—nonhuman primates are rather unlikely to have a capability for mental imagery (Hopkins, Fagot, and Vauclair 1993). Human children begin to handle mental rotation, slowly, around the four-to-five interval, and need several more years to increase its speed and become good at it (Lautrey and Chartier 1987; Newcombe and Huttenlocher 2006).

This later, slow development of productive mental imagery should be distinguished from the passive and reproductive ability of just having or dreaming mental images, or conjuring them up from memory. With a memory capable of retaining and storing what is visually perceived, young children and probably other animals can engage in reproductive but not productive imagery. This distinction echoes that (noted in section 3.1) between reproductive imagination and productive Imagination. The capacity for mental imagery that develops after four belongs to the latter.

Counterfactual thinking

Turning now to more abstract and nonimagistic thinking, the evidence suggests that close to age four, children also begin to handle offline future hypotheticals and a bit later counterfactuals as well. Yet as in the case of mental imagery, their progress is slow and takes several more years: the three- to four-year-olds can think of hypotheticals or (later) counterfactuals by setting aside their current knowledge, but they treat such alternatives in isolation, without connection to actual or other possible events. They do not seem able to maintain and contemplate several possible worlds at the same time. It is only around age six that children are able to recognize multiple and interconnected possibilities as genuine alternative worlds to be held in mind (Beck et al. 2006). This latter ability also turns out to be essential for Imagining.

Miscellanea

Other mental abilities, emerging in the four-to-five interval, are symptomatic of the onset of Imagination: reasoning about future and past states, making plans, delaying gratification, accurately reporting events of yesterday and tomorrow, and temporally differentiating events in the past and future (Bjorklund 2005; Suddendorf and Corballis 2007).

Somewhat more speculatively, other cognitive developments after four may also have a notable impact on the development of Imagination. One is the representational explicitation (or redescription) of what in younger years was cognized in a preeminently procedural mode and hence known only implicitly. Perhaps the best-known account of this developmental process is that of Annette Karmiloff-Smith (1992). Representational explicitation enables older children gradually to access consciously as well as verbally information that used to be domain specific and procedural, to re-represent it explicitly across several domains (physical, biological, formal, linguistic, etc.), modify and evaluate it, and subject it to explicit inferences. Imagination does all of these things, with explicitly constructed and represented thoughts and images.

The midchildhood development of the new mental abilities surveyed so far in this section is matched neurally by the concurrent development of the brain. Its progression in executive functions, which I will discuss more in a moment, and myelenation both continue well into the twenties and thirties, and are held responsible for significant advances in decision making, perspective taking, reasoning, and inductive thinking (Goldberg 2001; Luna et al. 2001). It takes some maturity to think well.

Patterns

What can be inferred from this brief survey of the growth of abilities associated with or symptomatic of the onset of Imagination? First, to risk a round number, the age of four seems to be a turning point. (Other estimates, somewhat more conservative, prefer the five-to-seven interval (Sameroff and Haith 1996).) If the abilities cited in this section have some systematic link with Imagination, either in a constitutive or enabling sense, then the emergence of those abilities around or after age four suggests that the same must be true of Imagination itself.

Second, advances in both the constitutive and enabling abilities of Imagination seem to proceed in a slow, somewhat uneven pattern. (As noted in the next chapter, imaginary companionship may fit this pattern, suggesting an earlier-than-average development of some of these abilities.) This uneven pattern would speak against a smooth organic maturation of a single competence.

This last point leads, third, to a critical question: Are these various abilities developing on their own, independently of each other, or in some sort of concertation, or are they resulting from the development of some common mechanism with variable applications? As far as I can tell, a conclusive answer is not in the cards at this time. Nevertheless, the next sections and next chapter may shed some light on this question, and also make some sense of the growth pattern just surveyed.

6.2 A New Executive

Motivation

The first item on the list of executive abilities drawn at the beginning of this chapter was the *intent* consciously and deliberately to engage in a specific act of offline Imagining. This is a less noticed yet most significant ingredient of Imagining. There are two sides to motivation in Imagination: one, external, is the motivation to Imagine at all, or to initiate this sort of mental activity; the other side, internal, is placing motivation in the *content* of what is Imagined. Both sides seem to develop only in midchildhood. The external motivation obviously accompanies the very capacity to Imagine.

The internal motivation is symptomatic of what can and cannot be Imagined. Internally, one envisages, say, a future state in which one's motivation (need, desires, or inclinations) is different from the current one. It turns out that until around age five, children have a hard time overriding their current motivation in order to envisage different needs, desires, or wishes in the future. Asked, for example, about preferring pretzels over water tomorrow, which they usually do, children younger than five prefer water, being currently thirsty after eating lots of pretzels (Atance and Meltzoff 2006). The same is true of selecting objects for future use, delaying gratification, or planning pleasurable activities in advance (Atance and Jackson 2009).

We hear, of course, of apes, birds, and other creatures anticipating future needs for food (caching) or tool use (carried to future destinations), independently of their current motivation. Are young children worse off on this score? This is not the place to debate this issue. As suggested in chapter 3, a plausible account of what those animals anticipate has less to do with their motivation than, most likely, with forward-looking *action schemes* cued by current inputs and relevant memories or acquired dispositions. Young children are not in a position—nor do they generally face existential pressures—to develop such action schemes. My reading of the comparative literature is that both animals and young children live in a motivational present (Shettleworth 2010; Suddendorf and Corballis 2007; Tomasello and Call 1997). That begins to change in human children after around age five, with major implications for the development of Imagining.

Multiple frames and cerebral novelties

To mark another dramatic contrast between the executive minds of children before and after age four, I will help myself to a serviceable metaphor (not to be read literally). According to this metaphor, infant minds before the age of one and a half to two operate in a single central frame, where various inputs from various modalities are displayed and constantly updated by new inputs. In the next two years or so, children's minds can open up multiple frames, cued and constrained by a current perceptual one, but tracking temporal changes or alternative situations, as in the fantasized variations typical of pretend play (Perner 1991).

What children younger than four apparently cannot do is completely *inhibit* and *quarantine* their current perceptual and motivational frames, construct alternative frames, and move mentally to the latter (as it were) by shifting perspective, adopting the new perspective of an alternative frame, and looking at and thinking about a possible world from that newly adopted perspective. Imagining is not possible without these mental moves, which go beyond just some partial offline operation, of which young minds are of course capable—for example, when told a story.

Inhibition and perspective shifting, alongside a vastly expanded working memory that can hold both the frame of ongoing mentation and those projected from alternative frames, are the chief executive acquisitions after age four with the most impact on the development of Imagination. But they are not the only ones; self-control, top-down attention, metacognition, and multitasking are also emerging after four (Bjorklund 2005; Sameroff and Haith 1996).

The chief *neural* platforms of this new executive mind are the (dorsolateral) prefrontal cortex along with the integrative connectivity handled mostly by the right hemisphere and reaching across large regions of the brain. The growth of these platforms is most dramatic in the four-to-six interval (Diamond 2001; Goldberg 2001).

Significantly, the self-regulatory range of the prefrontal cortex does not reach the sensory inputs and online capacities. This is to say that prefrontal self-regulation is massively *intramental*, as are the main mental activities that are regulated—

Imagining in particular. The independence from input and online transactions, fairly unique in animal mentation, means that the prefrontal executive has the flexibility to not only allocate and integrate resources across input-specific domains but also generate new domains, especially in Imagination.

All these cerebral developments liberate children's minds from the captivity of a perceptually and motivationally situated mentation as well as its current inputs, and enable them to entertain, often simultaneously and in different but interconnected mental frames, nested sets of alternative along with at times conflicting representations of actual and nonactual, current, past, and counterfactual facts and situations across various domains. This is what the mind of a genuine Imaginer can do.

It is still a big unsettled question why these cerebral developments, and why after age four. Alas, mental development during childhood is only rarely viewed through evolutionary lenses in the psychological and neuroscientific literature. I concur with Merlin Donald (2001) and David Bjorklund and Anthony Pellegrini (2001) that evolution installs not only content-oriented and domain-specific modules or capacities (the orthodoxy so far) but also resources, particularly executive, whose work is bound to be domain inspecific in order to be successful and adaptive. As a manager of mental frames, crucially involved in the work of Imagination, the prefrontal executive may actually be such an adaptive specialization responding to definite evolutionary pressures that cross domains. Linguistic communication, cultural learning, and sociopolitical interactions are the vital multidomain activities that older children increasingly engage in, relying massively on the prefrontal executive. These activities in turn would not be possible without the multidomain reach of children's intuitive psychology, which after four, increasingly turns inward as well, in a critical move toward Imagining.

6.3 Metarepresenting Others

Contrasts

As noted earlier in sections 2.4 and 4.3, during the first four years of childhood, the basic abilities of intuitive psychology in its bilateral and then naive versions—a sense of the mental in others, such as a recognition of emotion and intent, gaze and seeing, and simple desires and visually based beliefs—develop fairly uniformly and universally, according to what appears to be a well-sequenced schedule. This suggests the maturation of some underlying genetic predispositions. The deployment of these basic abilities, usually input triggered and tracking visible expressions of the mental states of others, seems to follow relatively straightforward rules or instructions, under appropriate recognitional categories. In short, this early bilateral and naive psychology has the marks of a rather instinctive enterprise, with a likely history of a probably lengthy natural selection (Bogdan 1997). In particular, it is from this platform that naive psychology contributes its grasp of intent, gaze direction and seeing, means–ends strategies, and shared attention to imitation. As a result, it enables young children to engage in pretend play, as argued in chapter 5.

Things change significantly after age four in both the nature and modus operandi of intuitive psychology. New and higher-power abilities develop. One of them is the ability to be aware of and interpret invisible mental states, and what and how they represent—an ability professionally called *metarepresentation*. It is central to setting up the suppositional stance, which in turn is central to Imagining. To see this, consider a brief exercise in Imagining.

While driving through a drab and glum part of town (there are plenty of those where I live), I Imagine myself vacationing on a sunny Greek island, with all the pleasant affordances and implications I can foresee. (In the current Greek crisis, I might even Imagine buying such an island, if I were better paid.) My Imaginative mind quarantines my current mentation toward the actual world from what is Imagined, takes the stance of my Imaginative thoughts, does not confuse what is Imagined with what is real yet takes what is Imagined seriously, though provisionally, in order to deploy further projections along with various predictions and anticipations. The abilities involved in this exercise in Imagination will be shown to originate in or at least depend on the initial work of metarepresentation in children's intuitive psychology, for reasons that are initially different from as well as earlier and more basic than those of Imagining.

There are significant and still unsettled debates about the nature and developmental timing of metarepresentation. Since my inquiry posits a crucial role for metarepresentation in setting up the suppositional stance and a similarly crucial role for the latter in the work of Imagining, a bit of critical footwork is in order.

Dissent

A wide consensus among developmental psychologists takes the capacity to *metarepresent* thoughts and attitudes to be at work in, and thus revealed by, children's ability to recognize false belief in others and themselves during the three-to-four interval

(Astington, Harris, and Olson 1988; Doherty 2009; Perner 1991; Wellman 1990) or even before (Leslie 1988), with some recent studies pointing even to infancy (Baillargeon, Scott, and He 2010).

I dissent. I think that metarepresentation develops somewhat later than the three-to-four interval and requires considerably more than what is involved in the early recognition of visually based false belief. The latter need *not* call for taking the perspective of another mind. Given that the beliefs tested in experiments with young children and surely infants are all formed *visually*, the recognition of their falsity may simply result from computing another person's visual access, or lack thereof, that person's memory retention of what was seen, or not seen, and predicting how that person may act—all of which are something that young children and possibly infants can do (Bogdan 1997, 2000, 2003; see also the appendix). In short, passing the visually based false-belief test need not require a capacity for metarepresentation (as I construe it).

Furthermore, I disagree with the consensual view that young children recognize the mental states of others and their own at the *same* time, with the *same* resources. I argued elsewhere that children recognize their own false beliefs (and other self-directed attitudes) later than they recognize the false beliefs (and other attitudes) of others, and do so with significantly different mental resources (Bogdan 2007, 2010; see also the appendix).

Without getting too exegetical here, I mention my points of dissent because, if the consensus were right, metarepresenting the attitudes of others and selves would develop simultaneously in the three-to-four interval. As a result, some basic tasks of Imagination and especially the suppositional stance could in principle be handled by children in that same earlier interval.

Yet as far as I can tell, there is no robust evidence to suggest that
(Bogdan 2010, chapters 2 and 3). Moreover, on my counting,
the three-to-four interval is still the age of online pretending
rather than offline Imagining, as also indicated by the evidence
reviewed in the previous two sections. I will have more to say
in the next section about metarepresenting one's own mental
states later than those of others.

Chapter 5 noted the view that pretend play already relies on
a suppositional stance. It is a view linked with the early timing
of metarepresentation (Leslie 1988). Other researchers link the
suppositional stance in pretend play to make-believe prompts
and joint pretendings (see, for example, P. Harris 2000, 2006). I
voiced my skepticism at that time about the operation of a suppositional stance in early pretending. I did acknowledge its
behavioral as-if stance and also the *let-us-play-mentally-together
stance* in acts of joint pretending, but I argued that these two
pretend stances do not amount to a suppositional stance. In
contrast, I think, offline and solitary Imagining, of one's own
volition, without the external inducements of play, social
prompts, and joint pretending, requires a *mental what-if stance*,
which I take to be a genuine suppositional stance, and which
develops later and builds on metarepresentation. With these
critical distinctions and clarifications on record, I will now
examine the role of metarepresentation in setting up the suppositional stance of Imagination.

The tasks
Any offline metamental rehearsal calls for a *mental* quarantine
of what is rehearsed from what is concurrently known and perceived to be real, a *suspension* of the truth-value, modal, and
doxastic status of what is rehearsed, and an adoption of the

perspective of a rehearsed projection as a basis for further projections and inferences. By "adopting the perspective," I mean aiming to visualize, image, or think *in terms of* that perspective, from its *angle*. These are, in my view, conditions jointly required by the suppositional stance. Older children's metarepresentation provides both the impetus and core mental equipment to do these things. Here is how, with the help of a little example.

Two five-year-olds, Tom and Alice, are playing together, when suddenly Alice's attention shifts to a little running animal. Tom realizes that Alice thinks she saw her cat run away, when in fact what she saw was a rabbit. Tom infers that Alice would run after the (misidentified) cat to bring it home. To explain or predict Alice's behavior, Tom's reasoning about Alice's behavior must separate what Tom knows about the actual situation (that it wasn't a cat) and *take* Alice's *perspective* on it. To do the latter, Tom must *quarantine* Alice's belief (and perspective) from his own and *suspend* its actual truth-value (as known to Tom). At the same time, to predict what Alice would do (run after the cat), Tom must take Alice's belief (that the animal is her cat) *as true for* Alice. These are all requirements of metarepresentation, as I construe it.

Being able to take the perspective of another mind means being able to make the mental moves just described, and bringing whatever information is pertinent to approximate how the other mind would perceive, image (verb here), remember, or conceptualize the situation to which it relates in some modality (visual, in my example). This goes beyond noticing and representing that another person represents some specific target (a fact or situation) in some modality (seeing, remembering, believing, etc.), which children younger than four can do. The condition requires that the metarepresenter also endeavors to figure out or approximate *under what terms and conditions* the other person relates to some concrete or abstract target. It is not success or fidelity that matters in this adoption of another's perspective, as it is rarely achieved fully, but rather the effort to approximate and the resources employed to do so. The basis of this approximation (evidence, shared knowledge, memory, generalizations, etc.) and how it is done (intuitive theorizing, simulating, modular grasp, etc.) are beyond the scope of my analysis. It is the approximation enterprise, as interpretation, that is at the heart of metarepresentation, after the age of four (Bogdan 1997).

This, succinctly, is how older children's suppositional stance builds on how they metarepresent other minds and their outputs (thoughts, attitudes, utterances, and actions). So far, it is an *extrovert* suppositional stance directed at *other* minds. There is abundant evidence that only after four, children begin to handle successfully the tasks involved in metarepresenting other minds and their outputs (Astington, Harris, and Olson 1988; Doherty 2009; Perner 1991). Since so analyzed, their suppositional stance cannot be operative earlier than age four to five, the same (based on my analysis) must therefore be true of their Imagination.

I will now change tack and try to reach this conclusion from another direction, in a devo-evo spirit. The question I ask is, What area of mental activity during preschool years, *other than* that of intuitive psychology patrolling the sociocultural and communicational domains, could possibly pressure or at least stimulate children to develop a suppositional stance? Where else, in what other domains, could the latter be indispensable to children's mental engagement with the world and their mental development? Is it in the physical, biological, or numerical domains? Not likely. In any of these domains, suppositional thinking will take literacy and schooling to develop, and still will be found difficult by many children and even adults. In contrast, suppositional thinking after age four gradually becomes universally easy and natural for practically everybody, *when thinking of other people, their mental states, and their situations.*

It may help to weave into this devo-evo argument a little true story that I find touchingly relevant. In the 1930s, Vygotsky's team conducted research in Soviet Asia to determine the impact of literacy on mental development. They found that illiterate adults had major difficulties reasoning conditionally from premises that were outside their experience. Told that in the snowy Far North all bears are white and Novaya Zemlya is in the Far North, those adults were asked about the color of the bears up there. Their answer to the principal investigator (Alexander Luria) was of the sort "You have seen them, you know. I haven't seen them, so how could I say?" Other, more explicit what-if questions received similar answers (Luria 1934).

This experiment suggested to its authors and other researchers that illiterate adults cannot take the suppositional stance (or "theoretical orientation" as it was initially called) toward unexperienced, unfamiliar facts and situations. At the same time, it was also found that the somewhat literate adults could be stimulated to focus on the wording of the conditional questions and draw the right conclusion. The general Vygotskian conclusion, later documented also among illiterate and literate adults in West Africa and Mexico, was that literacy makes the suppositional stance possible (P. Harris 2006).

As far as I know, the illiterate adults were *not* asked conditional or counterfactual questions in the *social* or interpersonal domain involving other people, with their *mental* states and behaviors. The argument of this section suggests that *if* asked such questions, the illiterate adults would have likely taken a metarepresentational stance similar to that of young Tom toward Alice in my earlier example. That would have amounted to adopting a suppositional stance in the social domain.

Revealingly in this respect, the illiterate adult's answer to the question about bears in the Far North was "You have *seen* them, you *know*. I haven't *seen* them, so how could I *say*?" (my emphases). It is an answer obviously and deliberately couched in intuitive-psychological terms, and drawing implicitly on relevant generalities, such as "seeing entails knowing" and "seeing enables asserting the truth." This intuitive-psychological formulation of the answer suggests a potentially metarepresentational take on the topic, which could have revealed more directly a suppositional stance, if the experiment's question were recast explicitly in intuitive-psychological terms. Intuitive psychology, however, was not on the agenda of psychological research in the 1930s.

The Vygotskian explanation that literacy helps in adopting a theoretical orientation rather than an observational or "empirical" one seems to me to indicate that literacy enhances the understanding of *syllogisms*—and perhaps reasoning, more generally—with unexperienced contents instead of bringing about the suppositional stance itself. I will not develop this distinction here, except to reaffirm the metarepresentational grounds of the latter.

Moving on, let us assume that in addition to the other acquisitions surveyed so far, the suppositional stance is metarepresentationally present in older children's minds along the lines just outlined—namely, oriented toward what and how *other* minds represent what they do. What exactly does this version of the

suppositional stance enable older children to Imagine? Synopti-
cally, the chief novelties it brings about are the following:

• suppositionally taking (or mentally inhabiting) the perspective of what is Imagined, and projecting and deploying further
thoughts (imagistic or abstract) from that perspective

• offline operation, often independently of current perceptual
inputs as well as current needs and motives

• content promiscuity, in the sense that the Imaginer can deliberately access, mix, and coordinate kinds of inputs and representations (images, abstract thoughts, gestures, and word
meanings) from a variety of sources as well as modalities, and
directed at a variety of domains

What the suppositional stance described so far, as a first
developmental version, *cannot* yet do is include the *self* with its
thoughts, attitudes (desires, beliefs, and intentions), and other
mental states (emotions and feelings) in the possible worlds it
projects. The sort of Imagination capable of such self-inclusion
is an inwardly oriented, introvert, or reflective Imagination. It
draws on new abilities such as

introvert Imagination

• an understanding and awareness that one's own Imaginative
thoughts are directed at or represent targets of interest (phrased
more technically, this is a conscious sense of the intentionality
or target directedness of one's own Imaginings), with the resulting ability to operate on this target directedness

• projection of a possible self (distinct from the current self of
the Imaginer) with its possible mental states in some possible
worlds, with full awareness of and control over this self-
regarding projection

How do older children develop these new abilities with inner-directed or introvert range, and why? The next section sketches an answer—not an exhaustive one by any means, just sufficiently suggestive of what enables introvert Imagination to take off.

6.4 Their Own Minds

It is fairly well documented that children need several good years after four to develop self-directed thinking, autobiographical memory, and introspection as well as introvert self-consciousness (Bjorklund 2005; Bogdan 2000, 2005b, 2007, 2010; Flavell et al. 1995; Nelson 1996; Piolino et al. 2007; Sameroff and Haith 1996). I think this is indicative of an equally slow and parallel development of their introvert Imagination. It is hard to think of the latter working normally in the absence of the former abilities.

What would explain children's turn toward their own minds? A devo-evo explanation in terms of the reasons why must await the next chapter. It suffices to say for now that publicly presenting the right image of self, justifying one's own thoughts and resulting actions, comparing one's own attitudes with those of others, and much more along similar lines are mental endeavors that older children are increasingly pressured to undertake for sociopolitical and cultural reasons, and these mental activities require a grasp and cognitive management, including rehearsal, of their own thoughts and attitudes.

What enables them to do so are several new abilities being formed gradually in midchildhood. Chief among them is a new form of intuitive psychology, which may be aptly called *commonsense psychology* precisely because it categorizes and (meta) represents one's own mental states in terms essentially (though not entirely) similar to those in which the mental states of others are categorized and (meta)represented. There are several accounts in the literature of what this commonsense psychology is and how it works. It is not important to get into the details here, as long as it is understood that commonsense psychology is a way of making common and mutually intelligible sense of minds in general. For the record, I favor a nearly Sellarsian line, reinterpreted in developmental terms, according to which, through a process of task emulation and transfer, children begin to think of their own thoughts and attitudes on the (metarepresentational) model of how they think of the thoughts and attitudes of others. This is an idea elaborated in detail elsewhere (Bogdan 2000, 2010), and I will enter it as a premise of the present argument.

What needs to be added and stressed here, because of its major role in the argument of the next chapter, is the fact that thanks to the new commonsense psychology, older children acquire a sense of a new Imaginable self, which is distinct from the current self, and whose mental states and actions can be projected across time, different domains, and various possible worlds. It will become the "projectable," even mentally "transportable" self, so to speak, that older children and adults can Imagine about.

To elaborate a little, we can distinguish *three* kinds of selves—two of them directly generated by distinct neuropsychological mechanisms. The *me-self*, which is the ownership version of self, results from the work of self-determining mechanisms that distinguish events inside an organism from events outside it. This is a basic determination of selfhood, perhaps best illustrated by the work of the immunologic and other internally self-regulatory mechanisms. The *I-self*, which is the agency or authorship version, results from the equally basic work of self-guiding mechanisms that initiate, monitor, and control an organism's relations to its environment. Finally, there is the *projectable self* or *P-self* that was just introduced in the previous paragraph (Bogdan 2010, chapter 7).

The me-selfhood and I-selfhood mechanisms normally work unconsciously, or little noticed. One may have a conscious sense of either when things go wrong. Dizziness can obscure the distinction between what happens inside and outside us, which is a temporary loss of me-selfhood. The schizophrenic symptom of thought insertion can be plausibly explained as a loss of mental agency or authorship of one's own thoughts, and hence a loss of I-selfhood.

The P-self is a quite different matter. Its projections are likely to be generated by a complex mental schematism developing after age four, which draws jointly on new abilities of introspection, inference, and particularly the metarepresentation of one's own thoughts and attitudes handled by the new commonsense psychology. Autobiographical memory is perhaps the best example of projection of a P-self with its past actions and mental states. It is documentably developing only after four (Conway 2002; Nelson 1996) and is conceptually intertwined with the development of metarepresentation (Perner 1991, 163–169; 2000; see also Bogdan 2010, 24–25, 44–46), which I also see developing after four. The self projected by autobiographical memory is distinct from the current I-self who does the projecting-as-remembering, and is metarepresented as related to actions, thoughts, and attitudes that are themselves related to their contents.

Autobiographical recall, I further argue in the next chapter (section 7.3), is a mental activity that has much in common with Imagining, both in the projection of a future, past, or possible self with its actions and mental states, the metarepresentation of the latter, and the deliberate and effortful (re)construction of what is recalled or Imagined, respectively. I would not exclude the possibility that it is the strategizing that develops in response to new sociopolitical pressures, as the new initial matrix and incubator of Imagination, that stretches children's minds projectively in the realms of the past as well as the future, or just the possible. Why and how this possibility becomes mental reality is the topic of the next chapter.

7 Imagining

Juvenile sociopolitics is what I call, in section 7.1, the new set of major and all-consuming challenges with which children are increasingly confronted after the age of four. For many though not all children, this intense interactivity with other children and adults outside family may, according to section 7.2, stimulate and facilitate the interesting phenomenon of imaginary companions—possibly an early harbinger of the paradigmatic adaptive response to the pressures of juvenile sociopolitics, which is strategizing. Even more symptomatic of the onset of Imagining, according to section 7.3, and using many of the same mental resources in comparable ways, is autobiographical memory, which emerges around the same time and for related reasons. An analysis of strategizing as the initial matrix and incubator of Imagination is undertaken in section 7.4. Finally, section 7.5 examines the conditions in which the multiply projective metamental rehearsals that implement strategizing in the sociopolitical domain are prone and likely to morph and diversify into a versatile, multidomain competence for Imagining.

7.1 New Challenges: Juvenile Sociopolitics

After age four, children begin to exit the warm, fairly routinized, and protective circle of the family (also tribe, in earlier times), and enter the more fluid, complex, surprising, challenging world of their peers and adult strangers. What was habitual, ritualized, and hence often implicit in the within-family interactions and communications is bound to require an effortful, more open-ended exercise in figuring out and reasoning about the minds of others, particularly other children outside the family circle. The new zeitgeist calls for complex interactions with others, collaborative as well as competitive. All this requires and rewards new mental skills with far-reaching interpersonal range.

Perhaps the most challenging mentally is what I call *peer sociopolitics*. Based on a variety of sources, from genetic to psychological and behavioral, Judith Harris (1995, 1998) has made a strong case for the decisive influence of peer interactions on the mental development of older children—an influence more decisive than that of parents, siblings, and the family environment in general. Induction into the peer group or peer socialization, as it may be called, requires, among other things, that aspiring children behave according to the rules of the group and share its attitudes. Through imitation and social learning, children begin to master the basic parameters of group affiliation—in-group favoritism, in-group coordination and cooperation, out-of-group hostility, within-group jockeying for status, and often hostility toward adults (especially in boys). To understand and master these parameters, and also negotiate new arrangements and relations, at times conflictual, with their own families, older children need new sociopolitical skills.

As sociologist Douglas Maynard argues, children are skillful politicians. Conflict is more prevalent in children's activities than in those of adults. Conflict and peer pressure make politics a children's specialty before it morphs into adult forms. So instead of thinking finalistically of children as future political adults and their political skills as preparing them for adult politics, it is more sensible to see political adults developing out of political children, and the latter's political skills as underpinning and morphing into those of the former. Maynard also notes that in peer contexts children deploy *specific* skills for offering or soliciting collaboration or solving conflicts. These are sociopolitical skills with which children handle "problems that are *local* to their play and work experiences" (Maynard 1985, 219; emphasis added).

I construe these specific and locally generated and operating skills as ontogenetic solutions to specific sociocultural and political problems. Their specificity and often datedness are further confirmed by the fact that the peer pressures of midchildhood diminish significantly when adolescents become adults and start families (J. Harris 1995). It is not that adult life is devoid of sociopolitical peer pressures (alas, no!); it's actually getting much worse. The point, rather, is that the peer-pressured sociopolitics of midchildhood calls for practices such as strategizing that end up installing the infrastructure for Imagination. When adults strategize, they can do it Imaginatively (which is why it can be worse), whereas initially the strategizing children can't, if my account is right.

Peer competition, of course, is not the only new form of interpersonal interaction for children after age four. Increasingly sophisticated communication, argumentation, and other discursive practices, cooperation in joint activities, long-term collaborations, alliances, and friendships, joint planning, conflict resolution, complex games and sports, and much more are as challenging and demanding, all pressuring for new interpersonal skills. This is why the wider phenomenon is juvenile sociopolitics—social as well as political.

At the same time, and most frequently within or in interaction with juvenile sociopolitics, children's induction into culture, communal practices and moral rules, and the folklore of the family, tribe, and nation continue apace. What becomes different from the enculturation of earlier years is the increasingly vicarious character of the symbolic transmission of culture from adults to children. The enculturation of young children was highly contextual, and done mostly by example, gesture, and pointed verbal expression. It was deliberately geared to direct and situated observation and communication as well as perceptuomotor assimilation and reproduction—hence ready for behavioral imitation. Pretend play reflects all these parameters.

After age four to five, however, this rather direct format of enculturation is gradually replaced by a symbolic format in which words, utterances, and public representations in general (e.g., stories, gossip, books, photos, and movies) have distant referents and invisible meanings. This new format of enculturation matches that of linguistic communication in general, and both, alongside juvenile sociopolitics, require an understanding of other minds. Quite often this is an understanding from a distance, so to speak, mediated by impersonal communication no longer anchored in a shared perceptual-and-action context, as it was in earlier years.

Juvenile sociopolitics and continuing enculturation are by far the most persistent, dynamic, multidomain, and hence challenging pressures children must handle after age four, involving most of their time, mental energy, and resources. As a result, the major mental solutions or even adaptations that children develop after four must be in response to these pressures. One mental-rehearsal practice at the threshold between early and later childhood seems to prefigure the switch to offline Imagining.

7.2 Transition? Imaginary Companionship

The question mark is meant to warn the reader that what follows is a matter of reasoned speculation that is not entailed or even sufficiently backed up by relevant evidence. The phenomenon is controversial and lacks a definitive explanation. Nevertheless, in the context of the present inquiry, it is interesting enough to deserve some attention, for, conceivably, it may not only fore-shadow Imagining but also its somewhat variable development and operation.

Around the age of three, and for several years, many (though not all) children project imaginary companions, in the form of personified dolls and other objects, but particularly friends and even their own selves playing an imagined role. It is not clear whether the role is imagined with a small *i* or capital *I*. That is the issue. Role impersonation in action seems to continue to be at the center of this projective exercise, in both interactions with others and private, perhaps as a follow-up of pretend play (P. Harris 2000; Taylor 1999; Taylor, Carlson, and Shawber 2007).

Pretending to interact with imaginary companions seems to be a more Imaginative exercise than pretend play with artifacts and typical roles, in the sense of chapter 5. To that extent, it may look as though fantasizing about imaginary companions marks a transition toward Imagination by showing signs of the latter still operating in the matrix of early pretending. More realistically, though, it may be to view imaginary companionship—as I will call it—as revealing signs of sociopolitical strategizing (and not yet Imagining itself), which in my analysis, is the precursor, initial matrix, and incubator of Imagining.

To elaborate, I take imaginary companionship to play two main functions: like pretend play, but in a more internalized fashion, it still rehearses metamentally sociocultural practices, especially by way of role impersonation; yet at the same time, it also begins to rehearse in a pretend envelope more individualized sociopolitical interactions with others, including somewhat unfriendly or "noncompliant" others (as they are called), thus anticipating the strategizing that emerges after age four.

Several features of imaginary companionship seem to vindicate this reading. To begin with, imaginary companionship takes off significantly later than pretend play, after age three, and is dominant during preschool years and even beyond— again much later than the life span of pretend play. Not all children practice imaginary companionship: the figures vary from two-thirds to three-quarters of the child population. This proportion, it seems to me, may begin to reflect variations in later strategizing and Imagining, with some children and adults definitely better at it than others. In contrast, pretend play appears to be fairly universal in spread and fairly uniform in performance.

That imaginary companionship gets closer to strategizing and only by implication Imagining (than did pretend play) is also confirmed by its coincidence with the development of inhibition, around age four, and the fact that children who engage in imaginary companionship show more inhibitory control than those who don't (Taylor, Carlson, and Shawber 2007). Inhibitory control is critically needed to engage in strategizing and later full Imagination. There are still other correlations that link imaginary companionship with strategizing. Children who have imaginary companions were found to be more sociable and have more advanced intuitive-psychological skills than children who don't have them. Reflecting these differences, preschool girls were found to be more likely to have imaginary companions than were boys (Taylor, Carlson, and Shawber 2007), and ordinary observation suggests that girls and later women are better intuitive psychologists than are boys and later men. Autistic children, generally failing on these counts, are not known to play the imaginary companionship game.

To sum up, imaginary companionship can be read as continuing the pretend-play policy of role impersonation in sociocultural action, but in less perceptuomotor and more offline terms, and envisaging more personalized rather than typical roles, thus anticipating the individualized sociopolitical interactions that become the main preoccupation of the next metamental-rehearsal practice of strategizing.

Whether my reading of imaginary companionship is right in speculating that it may prefigure strategizing, it is a well-documented fact that this phenomenon is almost contemporary with a dramatic "change of mind" that lays new foundations for older children's (and adults') mentation, leading up to Imagination, as argued in chapter 6. Some of the new foundational abilities may become operative in some children's imaginary companionship earlier than in the rest of the child population.

7.3   Clues from Autobiographical Memory

If imaginary companionship anticipates the strategic rehearsal of relations to other people, another remarkable and (again) uniquely human development, this time in memory, around the same age of four, has much in common with Imagining, from rationale to abilities involved and patterns of their deployment as double-projection metamental rehearsals. This form of memory, the autobiographical form, may indeed be assembled out of many of the same abilities as Imagining and for many of the same devo-evo reasons. There are many clues pointing in that direction.

The parallels

To see the significance of this parallel assembly in the same age interval and the light it can shed on the development of Imagining, it is important to extricate autobiographical memory from other forms of memory. One of these other forms is often mistaken for autobiographical.

Memory can be implicit and procedural (a know-how form) versus explicit and declarative or descriptive (a know-that form). Autobiographical memory is of the latter sort, as are the simpler and earlier developing versions of semantic memory of facts as well as episodic memory of past experiences. It is episodic memory that is often identified, wrongly, with autobiographical memory. The former is generally necessary but far from sufficient for the latter.

The main and decisive difference between episodic and autobiographical memory is that in the former one can (in the present, with one's current or working self) relive or reenact a past experience—say, the feel and imagery of it—without necessarily projecting a *past* self, distinct from the current one, and furthermore projecting this past self with its past mental states *in relation* to a past experienced content. Only the latter projections are autobiographical.

Infants and young children (as well as most animals) have semantic and episodic memories—that is, experience-based and experience-reenacting memories, respectively—but not autobiographical ones. Likewise in Imagining: it is not enough to project a possible experience—that could simply be an imaginative (small *i*) exercise, like in fantasy or daydreaming; in contrast, the hallmark of Imagining is the ability to project a future or possible self (distinct from the current one who does the Imagining) in relation to some future or possible experience, or some mental state and its content; the ability need not be always exercised in Imagining, but it should be there. The same is true of autobiographical recall: the past self and/or its past mental states need not always be projected autobiographically, but they could be, if needed.

Revealingly, it is only around age five that children begin to understand the temporal connection between a past and present self, and in general to connect past and present causally, and understand that mental states persist through time and can influence current behavior. Relatedly, not until five do children have a persistent stream of consciousness concerning internal states that allows them to track a continuous self through time (Fivush 2011).

What makes the difference? To begin with, it takes *metarepresentation* to represent a past self as *related to* (or representing) the content of a past experience or mental state in general. On my counting, as argued earlier in sections 6.3 and 6.4, metarepresentation develops only after age four and even later in a

self-directed way. Furthermore, to do metarepresentational projections, and also reenact past experiences and deploy inferences from such reenactments, one needs a capacious working
memory and other executive resources as well as some narrative
powers, all of which also develop after four (Bogdan 2010, 24–
25; Nelson 1996; Nelson and Fivush 2004; Perner 2000). The
same requirements were—and will be further—shown to apply
to Imagining as well.

The parallels between autobiographical recall and Imagining
don't stop here. Although it emerges around four, autobiographical memory is not fully consolidated and operational in all its
diverse applications until adolescence and early adulthood
(Fivush 2011; Nelson 1992; 1996, 162). The same is true of
Imagining. This should not be a surprise, since even in intuitive
terms autobiographical recall appears to be notoriously effortful,
inferential, and constructive, involving complex retrieval processes, which are in turn evaluated and further elaborated. All
this requires advanced executive and cognitive abilities. The
same is true of Imagining.

It is becoming increasingly clear that these parallels are not
fortuitous from a neuropsychological angle. On some accounts,
far from resulting from a maturation of neurocognitive functions, autobiographical memory is assembled out of a variety of
resources and skills, besides storage and recall, mixing primarily
cognitive and metasocial acquisitions (Nelson and Fivush 2004;
see also Bogdan 2010). I propose the same for Imagining. Revealingly again, unlike episodic memory, autobiographical memory
does not seem to have a dedicated brain location, yet the pattern
of diverse brain sites it activates overlaps considerably with that
of Imagining. The neural overlap of past and future event representations is indeed extensive, particularly during elaboration.

Every region engaged by the construction and elaboration of past events is also engaged by future events either to a similar or significantly higher level, in addition to regions specific to future events. As a consequence of this extensive overlap, the common network active during elaboration strongly resembles the network consistently documented in studies of autobiographical retrieval (Addis, Wong, and Schacter 2007; Bar 2007).

Autobiographical memory and Imagining also share basic deficits: those who are impaired in autobiographical recall also were found to be impaired in Imagining themselves in the future. Moreover, in healthy individuals, manipulations that reduced the specificity of past events (e.g., instructions or cues that induce a general retrieval style) also reduced the specificity of subsequently generated future events (Williams et al. 1996).

Why these parallels?

Having sampled these striking parallels and points of convergence, the burning question to ask is why—Why are autobiographical memory and Imagining so close in so many respects? One intuitive answer, that memory services adaptive behaviors in the future, is based on the following syllogism: one learns from experience in order to do well or better in the future; memory stores experiences that one projects in guiding future behaviors, so memory is for the future use of information. Imagination also projects into the future, hence its intimate link with (some form of) memory.

This syllogism is further vindicated by the relatively recent discovery (evoked in section 4.1) that projection is the default mode of the brain at all times. What is the brain going to project but experiences and patterns of relevant information accumulated and stored in memory (Bar 2007)? And why would the brain project them unless it is for use in further cognition and behavior in the future? As various analyses begin to suggest, even the mind-wandering and fantasizing versions of idle projection seem to underpin some preparedness for future thoughts and actions (Baird, Smallwood, and Schooler 2011).

Further questions

Notice, though, that these (why) explanations link projection, perhaps of the imaginative sort (small *i*), as in idle fantasizing, with memory in general. Yet my question here is, Why the intimate link between *autobiographical* memory and Imagining, and particularly why *after* the age of four? If memory in general provides stored material for future-oriented cognition, why does memory have to be *autobiographical* to vault the mind *Imaginatively*, and why do autobiographical memory and Imagining become linked, jointly operational, and gradually effective only after four? Or more basically, Why aren't semantic and episodic memories sufficient for learning from experience as well as predictions and even planning on that basis, as in most animal cognition?

Here are two further question-generating clues to the answer I propose in the next two sections. First, it appears that around three to four children are able to plan by way of self-projections into the future, ahead of their self-projections into the past (Fivush 2011). Assuming that it is indeed a distinct future self who is projected into the future, which is not clear, this asymmetry would suggest that projecting into the future is more important, and evolved earlier, than projecting a distinct self into the past, further strengthening the general notion that memory in general and its autobiographical version are *initially* for future-oriented projections. The implication would be that autobiographical memory and primarily the projection of a distinct self into the past may well be a by-product of projecting a distinct self into the future or some possible world. If so, why would that be? To cut the suspense, I think the answer may be found in the argument of the next section: strategizing as a common ancestor and stimulus for both Imagining and autobiographical memory.

Now the second but not unrelated clue: it turns out that the onset and growth of autobiographical memory is tightly linked neuropsychologically with older children's much more active fantasizing along with increasingly deliberate and elaborate acts of deception and lying (Ganis et al. 2003). Is there a reason for this tight link, if in fact there is one? And why specifically deception and lying, meshed with fantasizing? The next section tries to connect some of the dots in this emerging picture, and following some clues noted earlier, answer the questions generated by the intriguing phenomenon of autobiographical memory.

7.4 Strategizing

In a good devo-evo spirit, let me go back to the basics evoked at the outset of this chapter—the new and powerful challenges posed by juvenile sociopolitics after age four. How do older children respond to the new sociopolitical pressures of peer interaction, juvenile sociopolitics in general, and enculturation outside family? Imaginary companionship may mark the debut of an adaptive response: the relations to others enter imagination (probably still a small *i*) and possibly some timid offline metamental rehearsal. The onset of autobiographical memory tells us that a distinct self who is projected across time with its mental states and actions becomes possible as well as important.

But based on the account sketched conceptually in earlier sections (sections 1.1 and 3.3, and the introduction to chapter 6), there cannot be any genuine Imagining unless these novelties are factored by double projection into children's metamental rehearsals, which are the ones that treat thoughts about mental states as tool-like means to ends. What new sort of metamental rehearsals can do that?

My suggestion is that the adaptive response to the pressures of juvenile sociopolitics brings about a kind of metamental rehearsal by the double projection of thoughts and other mental states whose main function is to strategize, to put it in general terms. I construe *strategizing* as mentally figuring out and metamentally rehearsing offline how to handle the thoughts, attitudes, utterances, and actions of others, and in response, one's own. Differently said, strategizing is metamentally rehearsing offline how to reach one's goals by means of the *mental* states and actions of others, and also how to enable or influence others to reach their goals by means of the *mental* states and actions of oneself, either altruistically, cooperatively, or with ulterior selfish motives. It is primarily the mental states of others and oneself used projectively as means to ends that define strategizing, and in turn foreshadow Imagining.

Examples of strategizing, so construed, include: rehearsing what to say and what to do; thinking how others think of you; planning how to relate to others and how to react to their reactions; deliberate and planned lying or obfuscation; gossip, including self-involving gossip; elaborate stories or communicative exchanges mixing reports of one's mental states with those of others; justifying publicly one's motives, reasoning, and actions; autobiographical recitations; fantasizing about what one could do in the future in relation to others; self-evaluation and criticism as well as self-advertising; defending one's opinions; interpersonal diplomacy; and many other exploits along the same lines.

These sorts of mental activities occupy the minds of older children, adolescents, and adults a good deal, if not most, of their waking hours. Ordinary observations and professional investigations concur that such mental activities enter the repertory of children after age four, and that their exercise improves gradually (Bjorklund 2005; J. Harris 1995; Maynard 1985; Mercier 2011; Nelson 1996; Perner 1991; Riggs and Beck 2007; Rogoff 1990; Sameroff and Haith 1996).

Since strategizing is assigned such a critical role here in children's mental development after four, it is worth reflecting (briefly) on its apparent novelty.

Precursors?

Strategizing may seem to be within the mental reach of nonhuman primates, particularly chimpanzees. After all, purposeful deception is something they often do. Their acute sense of social relations (e.g., who is friend or enemy with whom, who helped whom in the past, who is sincerely or tactically grooming whom, and so on) and political roles (e.g., who is alpha male or dominant and who is not, who is likely to challenge the alpha male, and so on) enables them to tactically pursue their goals by means of others (Byrne and Whiten 1988; Tomasello and Call 1997; Whiten 1991).

Strategizing may seem not entirely beyond the mental powers of children younger than four, either. They often cry or create tantrums pretendingly in order to get what they want. Even their pretend play is frequently used to please an adult or befriend a child partner in order to get something desired.

Three-year-olds can also lie as well as actively engage in deception by playing tricks on unsuspecting victims (Bjorklund 2005, 246; Polack and P. Harris 1999). They can also produce simple arguments that further their goals in negotiations with others or when justifying their actions (Mercier 2011).

Such facts are not in dispute. My (admittedly) informal notion of strategizing, however, involves more that merely reaching one's goals by means of others, no matter how clever the means. Crucially, strategizing also involves deliberate, effortful, and explicit *offline* and *metamental* rehearsal about the beliefs, intentions, expectations, and other *mental* states, of others and oneself, when (most of the time) these states are *not* behaviorally manifested and thus observable. As I read the evidence, the apparently strategic thinking of apes and young children is neither offline nor about beliefs, intentions, and other such inferable mental states. This difference is crucial to what follows, so I will briefly recapitulate the reasons for it.

Although different in motivation and resources, the apparently strategic thinking of apes and young children has this much in common: it is online and perceptually situated, input- and context-driven (lacks generality), anchored at a present time along with a current and online sense of self, driven by current motivation and emotion, also caused by current stimuli and memories, and attends solely to the perceptually accessible relations and behaviors of conspecifics, or between conspecifics and the world, as exhibited by gaze, simple desires revealed by observable goals and interests, discernible emotions, bodily postures, and actions.

In light of this analysis, apes do not look like offline strategizers, in the sense adopted here. Their thinking is unlikely to develop into Imagination, given that the latter requires the mental resources I am suggesting here. As of now, I know of no credible evidence that apes have such resources. Young children of course have the potential to develop Imagination, but if my earlier analysis is right, in the first three to four years their minds are run by abilities that respond to other dominant pressures, especially those generated by the assimilation of the visible culture and shared language. I take online pretending (as analyzed in chapter 5) to reflect young children's mental responses to these pressures.

Strategizing is a mental activity that adults engage in with gusto and are fairly uniformly good at (signs of a universal competence). Older children gradually master strategizing, in synchrony with the executive and cognitive developments envisaged by my hypothesis. If strategizing is the main form of offline metamental rehearsal that children undertake in response to the new sociopolitical challenges confronting them after the four-to-five interval, then the question my inquiry should ask is what mental *tasks* are involved in strategizing. The analysis of the tasks in turn can tell us what mental abilities strategizing is likely to recruit, assemble, and use to be effective. This tasks-to-abilities analysis will be shown to vindicate the novelty of the abilities involved (surveyed in chapter 6). It will also vindicate the role of strategizing, under sociopolitical pressures, in orchestrating and deploying these new abilities in patterns that will became templates for as well as incubators of Imagining.

Strategic lying

A concrete and familiar example may best intuitively convey the gist of my analysis. Deliberate, planful, metamental, and reflective lying is representative of strategizing; it is also familiar and thus easy to understand, and strikingly novel among the mental activities of older children (Ganis et al. 2003; J. Harris 1998; Maynard 1985). For the purposes here, I will call this novel form of lying *strategic lying* and distinguish it from simple lying, of which, as already noted, young children are fully capable.

Some psychologists see a gradual continuity between simple and strategic lying, as they may see a gradual continuity between animal deception and simple lying. In the same vein and for some of the same reasons, some psychologists (including a reviewer of this text) see a more general continuity between playful pretending and Imagining. As should be clear by now, I do not see such a gradual and organic continuity, based on my reading of the extant evidence, but particularly in the larger-picture view (evoked in section 3.2) that considers interacting patterns of executive and cognitive abilities that are systematically (not just occasionally) deployed in response to intense and pervasive challenges in specific periods of childhood.

Children younger than four are known to engage in simple lies and deception either by withholding information, destroying evidence, or providing misleading information (for a survey, see Bjorklund 2005, 254–255). Some researchers think that three-year-olds are able to solve the false-belief task when actively tricking another person, thereby suggesting a link between deception and metarepresentation (Sullivan and Winner 1993). This interpretation has been contested (Peskin 1992; Sodian et al. 1991). Yet even if children younger than four can solve the false-belief problem with means simpler than metarepresentation (as argued in Bogdan 2003, 2010; see also section 6.3 and the appendix), their solution need not involve metarepresentation and hence the ability to adopt the mental perspective of others, both of which are required for strategic lying and later Imagining. In the larger-picture view, in addition to the offline deployment of metarepresentational capabilities directed at other minds and one's own, strategic lying (but not simple deception and simple lying) would also require inhibition, a capacious working memory, top-down metacognitive control, introspection, introvert self-consciousness, and more— all of which are undeveloped or underdeveloped in younger children.

I conclude, then, that strategic lying and strategizing in general are not within the reach of the minds of apes or children younger than age four, nor do strategic lying and strategizing develop gradually and organically out of apparent precursors such as simple lies and deceptions. I trust that the analysis that follows will reinforce these conclusions.

The tasks of strategic lying

It so happens, luckily, that an insightful study about children's lying by Susan Leekam (1991; see also Leekam's research reported in Perner 1988) provides a good empirical context for my analysis. To begin with, the study confirms that children recognize and engage in deliberate, effortful, and planful—hence strategic—lying only after age four. It also supports the notion that such lying—and I would add, strategizing in general—begins on a prereflexive and extrovert note, without factoring in explicitly one's own mental states, and is deployed without much thematic connectivity. Introspective reflexivity, self-directed metarepresentation, and thematic or narrative connectivity take some years to develop. One can plausibly suspect a similar development of children's Imagination.

Furthermore, the ability to ascribe and recognize second-order mental states (such as beliefs about beliefs), which is essential to strategic lying, also develops around five to six, and the ability to distinguish more thematically connected or narrative intentional falsehoods, such as teasing, jokes, and sarcasm, from simple lying seems to develop still later, around eight (Perner 1988). Again, these fragments of evidence suggest that the development of Imagination is likely to follow a rather similar pattern and schedule.

To mark this parallel between the ontogenesis of strategizing, illustrated by its lying version, and Imagining, I will parse the analysis of the contributing abilities into executive and cognitive, with the latter mostly of the intuitive-psychological sort, and to ease the reader's visual processing, I will italicize the former and capitalize the latter. Together, the italics and capitals literally emphasize the main joints of strategic lying, which (based on my analysis) reflect abilities that inhabit and run strategizing in general, and will morph into the core mental machinery of offline Imagination.

I propose to sequence the analysis in stages, such as extrovert unmentalized, then extrovert mentalized, and finally introvert mentalized, which (again premised on my analysis) reflect significant stages in the development of the offline metamental rehearsals running children's strategizing and later Imagining. (*Mentalized* means here representing mental states.) In other words, this developmental sequencing is specifically about how children's lying is likely to become fully strategic gradually, but also, more generally and more important, how their strategizing and Imagining are likely to develop after age four. So here I go, somewhat pedantically.

To tell a strategic lie, resulting (after careful preparation) in saying or somehow conveying that not-p, when actually p is the case, one (an older child here) must be able to *extrovert and unmentalized*

• know that p is true and not-p false (factual knowledge) but

• *intend* to lie, as trigger of a complex mental activity

• *combine* thoughts and other mental states *from several modalities* (perception, memory, communication, etc.)

• *actively search memory* for the right information to be used in the lie

• *mentally plan and rehearse* the plot of the lie and its implications

• exercise *top-down attention, metacognitive* awareness, and *control* over the construction and delivery of the lie

This was the *executive* side—actually only a part of it, as will be noted shortly. It can also be noted, rather abstractly, that these executive abilities are in principle available to those children younger than four who envisage imaginary companions—abstractly, because (in my counting) their intuitive psychology is still in a naive mode geared to the visible and behaviorally expressed attitudes of others, whereas strategizing requires the more powerful and introvert intuitive psychology of the commonsense sort, as mentioned later.

To tell a strategic lie, one must also be able to

extrovert and mentalized

• INTEND to produce in someone else the BELIEF that not-p (this is an elaborate, topically focused and representationally formed intention to produce a particular belief in an audience, and to that extent, is different from and richer than the initial executive intent just to lie)

• KNOW that by lying one is doing something wrong (a public standard that children initially and even adults are prone to

construe in terms of the inferred ATTITUDES of others [e.g.,
what others would think about lying])

• but THINK of some justification (likely to be construed in
terms of one's goals related to—say, influencing—the ATTI-
TUDES of others)

Psychological research shows that in the four-to-six interval
children begin to successfully handle the executive and intuitive-psychological tasks just surveyed (Astington and Gopnik
1988; Doherty 2009; Leekam 1991; Mercier 2011; Perner 1988,
1991; Zelazo et al. 1999). Still lacking in strategic lying in the
same age interval are placing the *self* in the picture, with its
mental states (self-reflexivity), and a thematic connectivity that
would weave together other minds and their actions with one's
own, in a connected and coherent narrative of selves, others,
and the world. A strategic liar (and later an offline Imaginer)
therefore must also be able to factor in the *self*, and make reflexive or self-directed ascriptions of attitudes and other mental
states—that is, be able to

introvert and mentalized

• KNOW$_s$ that one KNOWS that p is true and not-p is false

• KNOW$_s$ that one has this INTENTION with this means–ends
effect on someone else's BELIEF

• THINK$_s$ of some self-justification in terms of one's own ATTI-
TUDES and other MENTAL STATES

The s-subscripted capitals now refer to self-directed thoughts
and attitudes, or briefly, self-thoughts and self-attitudes. Self-
thoughts and self-attitudes depend on self-directed metarepresentation, which is delivered by a self-directed commonsense
psychology through self-ascriptions of attitudes and other

mental states. It follows that a self-thinker, which a strategic liar is (as is a fully developed offline Imaginer), must also be able to

• explicitly METAREPRESENT$_s$ what one's own thoughts and attitudes are about (their target relatedness), and their affordances or implications

Yet self-attitudes and self-thoughts cannot be produced and managed unless one is also *executively* able to

• *introspectively access* one's self-thoughts and self-attitudes as being one's own as well as self-regarding

• monitor *metacognitively* what one is doing with self-thoughts and self-attitudes

• exercise *intentful control* over the self-thoughts and self-attitudes involved in the lie, and over their affordances or implications for others and the self

And given that strategic lying requires context-sensitive thinking as well as communication and reaction, one must also be able to

• *manage narratively* the thematically connected and coherent rehearsal along with delivery of the lie, and adjust it to the context and reactions of the lied-to person and others

As homework, readers are invited to produce their own example, either from autobiographical memory or some recent exposure to an instance of strategic lying. In so doing, readers may check the example against the list of conditions just surveyed. If some of the conditions are not met, it only means that the illustrated lying is not strategic enough.

Let me make one brief remark about the last condition. The complex ability of the narrative management of strategic lying, strategizing in general, and later Imagining grows out the lengthy development of the capacity to narrate, whose full mastery is reached only in adolescence (Bruner and Feldman 1993; Nelson 1996; see also Bogdan 1997, chapter 7). Some researchers, such as Paul Harris (2000) and a reviewer of this text, see young children's ability to comprehend and follow narratives as indicative of Imagination, and alongside it, their ability to produce narratives as driving the development of Imagination.

I have not attempted here to analyze the general competence for narration—not even its relation to Imagination. The present focus was on the infrastructure of Imagination, particularly on doubly projective metamental rehearsals about mental states, instead of the various interactions with other mental competencies, as required by narrations. I suggested at the end of the chapter on pretend play (in section 5.6) that young linguistic narrativity draws on script narrativity, often reenacted in pretending. Script narrativity does not look (to me) genuinely Imaginative, as it fails most of the conditions just examined in strategic lying. The fact that young children can understand and follow (simple, unsophisticated) narrations offline may suggest that elements of the narrations trigger appropriate memories, mental images, and other associations, and need not indicate that the mental projections involved also meet the conditions associated with strategizing and hence Imagining.

Indeed, I suspect (but have not argued here) that the relation between narrativity and Imagining may develop along two tracks. On one track, the basic tools of full offline linguistic narrativity, exercised in both comprehension and production, are likely to draw on the prior and more basic development of strategizing, and thus the development of the infrastructure of Imagination, rather than the other way around. On the other track, linguistic narrativity not only stimulates, enriches, and expands the powers of Imagination but also is likely to shape the patterns in which the basic tools are deployed. Ubiquitous gossip is as good an example as any of the interaction of these two tracks: it constantly and cheerfully deals with mental projections of thoughts about mental states, along the dimensions of strategizing evoked in this section (the basic tools), but also deploys these projections in more or less narrative patterns. The present inquiry has focused on the first track and the basic tools it generates, which it deems the more fundamental. For lest we forget, people are generally much better strategizers than narrators, and variability in strategizing is much narrower than that in narration, which suggests that strategizing may be closer than narration to being a basic ontogenetic solution or even adaptation.

7.5 Competence Transfer

The conceptual profile of strategizing, illustrated with strategic lying, was meant to identify—in a tasks-to-abilities analysis— key executive and cognitive (mostly intuitive-psychological) joints of offline metamental rehearsals with thoughts about mental states, which (based on my hypothesis) will morph into the core infrastructure of offline Imagination. Differently said, those executive and cognitive joints will provide the initial matrix and incubator of that infrastructure. This means that children *initially* Imagine offline because—and pretty much in the same ways in which—they strategize about the mental states of others and their own.

  Is there a plausible way to determine that strategizing is indeed the ontogenetic incubator and initial matrix of the infrastructure of Imagination? In other words, can it be shown that the abilities that run the former end up mutatis mutandis running most of the latter as well? To put it as modestly as I can, I think a positive answer is within the realm of plausibility.

As I see it, the required demonstration has three parts. The conceptual component shows a near isomorphism between key parameters of strategizing and Imagining. The empirical part displays the temporal lockstep in which the two develop. The third element, for which I do not have a handy adjective, shows that the deployment of projective thoughts about mental states, treated as tools in the means–ends format of strategizing, lends itself to Imaginative generalization beyond the initial sociopolitical range of strategizing.

The first conceptual part proceeds in several steps, some already made. Step one was to provide a conceptually intuitive and phenomenologically accessible profile of offline Imagination. I did this in the beginning of chapter 6 and intuitively at the outset in section 1.1. Step two was to articulate and illustrate the main joints of offline metamental rehearsal with thoughts about mental states, as in strategic lying. I just concluded this step in the previous section. A quick comparative look at the two steps shows a remarkable match between the executive and cognitive abilities involved in Imagining and strategizing (in its lying version).

The third step, which I am about take, mixes the conceptual and empirical, and consists in identifying several defining respects in which the two sides to be compared—strategizing with thoughts about mental states and offline Imagining, respectively—are related in significant ways or share a significant core. These defining respects are the domains of the two competencies, the resources they employ, their modes of operation, their developmental schedules and the comparable variability of as well as deficits in their exercise.

This list of shared respects is not exhaustive, but it can be fairly conclusive. I will phrase these shared respects in general terms and then indicate their presence in the discussion that follows. In developmental terms, which are of interest here, metamental rehearsal practices (such as, in this case, strategizing) are treated as the precursor competencies or initial matrices, and what they beget (offline Imagining and other intellectual faculties, as the case may be) are treated as the successor faculties. So here I go.

DOMAINS: the precursor competence systematically represents targets (i.e., entities, relations, and situations) in various domains in ways that are systematically similar to the ways that the successor competence represents in its domains

Discussion: The domain criterion is satisfied, because strategizing is about possible scenarios involving not only other people but also their thoughts and attitudes, with their contents as well as actions. Offline Imagination in general is also about possible scenarios, often in the same psychological domains but also in others (technology, art, science, education, and so on).

Furthermore, the domain versatility of strategizing can plausibly explain that of Imagination. This is because the strategizer's intuitive-psychological probes into the minds of others and one's own reach mental contents that usually range over a variety of domains, usually different from the surrounding context of the strategizer or the realm of mental states altogether. This domain versatility, generated initially by thinking strategically of the thoughts, attitudes, and actions of self and others, with contents in various domains, is (I conjecture) what offline Imagination inherits from strategizing.

To generalize, I think this is one plausible way to handle the puzzle of the domain versatility of the intellect. As a battery of domain-specific abilities, children's commonsense psychology is bound to track the various domains represented by the mental states of others and oneself, and to that remarkable extent, commonsense psychology is central to the evolutionarily novel and unique propensity of the human intellect to cross as well as combine domains creatively. And the reasons for the domain versatility of commonsense psychology are to be found in a sociocultural and sociopolitical ontogeny of older children.

RESOURCES EMPLOYED: the precursor competence and its successor share sufficiently many essential resources employed in their exercise

Discussion: To do their respective jobs, both strategizing and Imagining call on such executive resources as projecting, intending, quarantining, metacognizing, top-down attention, and control, and such cognitive resources as supposing, metarepresenting, introspecting, and more, down the lists envisaged earlier in this chapter.

MODE OF OPERATION: the shared resources are similarly deployed, in the sense that the precursor competence operates executively and cognitively in metamental-rehearsal patterns that are close, if not similar, to those of the successor competence

Discussion: Here is an illustrative sample of a parallel exercise of abilities. To Imagine/lie strategically is to know that what one Imagines/lies is not actual; intend to Imagine/lie as a trigger to a complex mental activity; combine thoughts and other mental states from several modalities; actively search memory for the right information; deliberately and explicitly plan and meta-mentally rehearse with thoughts treated as means to ends; exercise top-down attention, control, and metacognition over the Imagining/strategizing activity; exercise self-knowledge of what one is doing mentally; know metarepresentationally that one's Imaginative/lying thoughts are directed at or represent possible states of affairs; and adopt a suppositional or what-if stance toward what is Imagined/lied about.

DEVELOPMENTAL TIMING: the precursor competence not only predates its successor competence but also cannot develop until the resources that contribute to both competencies develop as well, in the same temporal order

Discussion: Strategizing develops only after the four-to-five interval and so does Imagination—the former faster and somewhat earlier than the latter. Key executive and cognitive resources for both strategizing and Imagining, such as inhibition, quarantine of current input, and a capacious working memory, among others, as well as metarepresentation and supposition, also develop only after the four-to-five interval.

VARIABILITY AND DEFICITS: variations in the development of the precursor competence along with its more basic and earlier contributors are reflected in variations in the development of the successor competence; the same could be true of deficits in the former that are reflected in the latter

Discussion: The empirical evidence is suggestive but less robust here. There are variable estimates of the onset of some of the earliest contributors to intuitive psychology, such as shared attention (at nine, twelve, or eighteen months), metarepresentation (at three to four years old, or as I think, even later), self-directed attitude ascriptions (at four to six years old), and more. This variability may reflect methodological differences in what is measured and how, but may also reflect different rhythms in the mental developments in question. If the latter, as I am inclined to believe, then the relatively variable development of these early resources may be reflected to some extent in the somewhat variable development of, say, strategizing and Imagining. Imaginary companionship was earlier conjectured to reflect such developmental variability.

On the deficits side, the much-used (and abused) example of autism is again suggestive: many and perhaps most autistic children fail to develop, or sufficiently develop, some basic resources of the intuitive-psychological sort, such as shared attention, metarepresentation, and self-directed attitudes, and are known to be poor strategizers and poor Imaginers.

The last several paragraphs, when joined to the rest of this chapter and the previous one, contribute to the second, empirical part of the demonstration, which is to show that the development of the abilities for strategizing predate but are in close age proximity and likely operational lockstep with the ascertainable manifestations of children's growing Imagination.

Finally, I come to the third step of the demonstration, only briefly gestured at here. Sections 2.2 and 3.3 introduced the notion of thoughts treated in conscious, deliberate, and effortful metamental rehearsals as *mental tools* causally manipulated as means to reach one's desired ends. It was noted then that it is in the nature of tools, so manipulated, to be improved, modified, linked to other tools, and used in new applications in new domains for new purposes in a sort of "ratchet effect" (in the sense of Tomasello 1999). Education, imitation, indoctrination, and in general cultural evolution can not only bring physical tools, conventional behaviors, and cultural practices under the ratchet escalator but also *mental* activities and ways of thinking, such as Imagining. This means that once the competence for strategizing is firmly in place, as a matrix of thinking about other people and their minds in the sociopolitical domain, then education, culture, and other influences can later improvise new deployments of the matrix in new domains, in combination with new abilities and various databases, leading to the formation of new faculties—not just Imagination, but also new intellectual applications. Furthermore, the variability of the shaping influences (education, culture, and so on) as causes of this ratchet escalation in the realm of the mind can, in a large measure, explain individual variability in the exercise of intellectual faculties, beginning with Imagination.

Returning to the parallel evoked two sections ago, autobiographical memory itself, with its distinct self along with mental states and actions projected in the past, may be construed as resulting from the development of strategizing and the ratchet escalation it generates. This is because effective strategizing requires not only appropriate projections of a distinct self along with its mental states and actions into the future or possible situations (the argument of the previous section) but also making the past self and its mental states compatible, if not congruent (or harmonious), with the current and future-projected selves and their mental states. In this sense, autobiographical recall is an exercise in coherence and continuity—the rich personal identity we all strive for—initially dictated and stimulated by the same sociopolitical reasons as those for strategizing. But this is just an opening for further thought.

Thus concludes my inquiry into the reasons for and roots of—or grounds for—mindvaulting as pretending and Imagining. Given that Imagination, as construed here, is the engine of the intellect, the devo-evo analysis undertaken in this book may shed some preliminary light on how to go about explaining other quarters of the intellect in the same methodological spirit. The epilogue, next, ventures some thoughts in this direction.

8   Epilogue

8.1   Summation

The traditional notion and label of *intellect* were revived here to include such higher mental faculties as reasoning, deliberate planning, thoughtful communication, reflective problem solving and decision making, art creation, technological innovation, and scientific theorizing. At the heart of these faculties—their shared core—is what I labeled *mindvaulting*, and described as the consciously and deliberately exercised ability of the human mind to vault itself out of the enclosure of current perception, motivation, emotion, and action, and leap over to future, past, possible, or even impossible facts, situations, or scenarios.

The intellect in general and its mindvaulting core in particular were said to be puzzling in many ways. They are phylogenetically unique, since present only in human minds, and apparently evolved rather recently, only in modern humans. Yet even for modern human minds, the intellect and its mindvaulting capacities are puzzling because it is not obvious why they evolved and under what selection pressures. Their basic properties, such as domain versatility, nonmodularity, and high interactivity among faculties as well as significant variability of use, do not point to any definite selection pressures and hence resist standard evolutionary explanations. The lack of dedicated genetic bases and dedicated brain sites as well as their hierarchical compositionality, gradually built up during ontogeny, add further puzzles to the list.

As a resolution to these puzzles, I proposed to reorient the inquiry toward modern human ontogeny as an environment of evolution sui generis, with its unique selection pressures and unique adaptive responses to such pressures. In this new explanatory framework, which I construe as developmental evolution or devo-evo, mindvaulting and more generally the intellect appear as outcomes of a unique ontogeny. What makes human ontogeny unique, and can plausibly explain mindvaulting, are primarily its sociocultural and later sociopolitical pressures.

I distinguished two initial forms of mindvaulting as adaptive responses: cultural learning through role impersonation in response to early sociocultural pressures, and strategizing in response to later sociopolitical pressures. What they have in common operationally are conscious, deliberate, and effortful metamental rehearsals by double projection, which treat thoughts about mental states as tool-like means to ends. The metamental rehearsals that run cultural learning through role impersonation and strategizing assemble a variety of available abilities that develop initially for a variety of reasons in a variety of domains, ranging from projection, imitation, and naive psychology in early childhood to new executive abilities along with a metarepresentational commonsense psychology in later childhood. Cultural learning through role impersonation and strategizing become the initial matrices and incubators of the resulting major versions of mindvaulting: pretending and Imagining.

The largely distinct pressures calling for definitely distinct forms of metamental rehearsal, assembling vastly different abilities, strongly suggest that Imagining is an adaptive ontogenetic solution largely independent of pretending, but crucially helped along by the sociocultural and mental acquisitions that the latter brings about. Intuitive psychology is the fulcrum competence that turns projections into metamental rehearsals and the latter into distinct forms of mindvaulting. Imagining alone becomes the heart and engine of the human intellect.

8.2 Speculation

To add a speculative note to what was argued so far, the preface mentioned that the crania of modern humans are higher than those of archaic humans (and apes), and that paleoanthropologists call the difference *vaulting* and suspect its possible link to modern human minds. The present inquiry suggests that this cranial vaulting in modern humans may plausibly be credited to a new (modern) human ontogeny, and in particular its executive and cognitive (mostly intuitive-psychological) developments after the four-to-five interval—hence to factors that contributed essentially to the onset and development of Imagination.

One intriguing implication here would be that prior to the modern revolution in human ontogeny, possibly during the last hundred thousand years or so, archaic humans (maybe including the last group, the Neanderthals) may have largely operated mentally with the organically matured versions of most of the executive and cognitive abilities of *young* modern children, up to around the age of four or so—the pretending but pre-Imaginative children of this book. These abilities would have included a basic language (gestural or verbal) yet not a pragmatic discourse of any significant sophistication, a basic naive (but not commonsense and introvert) psychology and other naive forms of domain-specific expertise (physical, biological, numerical, etc.), semantic and episodic although not autobiographical memory as well as playful pretending in the service of basic forms of cultural learning by role impersonation.

What may have been lacking in the minds of archaic humans, according to this admittedly speculative evolutionary scenario, was Imagination and its generalization to an intellect as the übervault of the human mind. Modern human adults may have acquired higher crania and became intellectuals because as well as when their older children became Imaginative, for the reasons and with the resources canvased in this book.

Going beyond its thematic and speculative confines, the inquiry just concluded raises the more general question of whether the devo-evo argument about Imagination proposed in this book might help rethink the nature and evolution of the intellect along with the way cognitive science studies the intellect as well as many other cognitive competencies. The following are some parting thoughts occasioned by this question.

8.3   Why Evolution Matters

The argument of this book could not be right or close to plausible, or at the very least worth considering, if it hadn't taken evolution seriously and specifically applied to ontogeny as developmental evolution. The various puzzles evoked in chapter 1, the uniqueness of modern human ontogeny, the surprising behaviors of apes in cultural captivity, the overwhelming predominance of sociocultural and sociopolitical pressures in the first years of life along with their mighty impact on the growing human minds, the resulting importance of regulative genes and epigenetic markers, and the real possibility, under their guidance, of an assembly of initial matrices for metamental rehearsals that later develop into high-power faculties, such as Imagination—all these topics, central to the argument of the book, would not make much sense without a devo-evo stance on them. Yet that stance is not so obviously plausible or useful in light of the still dominant tradition in cognitive science.

The classical cognitive science, initiated and progressing since the 1950s under the mighty impact of the two Cs—Chomsky and the computer metaphor of the mind—has notoriously shunned evolution. It did so not because its distinguished pioneers and most other practitioners were against evolution (they were not) but instead because they thought, first, that most evolutionary explanations were speculative (just-so stories!), and second and even more important, because the mental capacities best studied, such as grammar and vision, were successfully theorized about and explained without appeal to evolution. In short, where classical cognitive science was most successful, evolutionary explanations appeared either too speculative or simply unnecessary, if not redundantly irrelevant.

Grammar, vision, and a few other mental capacities are modular, and as Jerry Fodor (1983) phrased it in his crisp and influential *Modularity of Mind*, classical cognitive science knows how to think of cognitive modules: the modules have properties that classical cognitive science can do explanatory business with—sans evolution, thank you.

Actually, this is not quite accurate. In a book published many years ago, I suggested a convergence between modularity and the standard work of natural selection: the latter tends to install specialized mechanisms and organs, which is exactly what cognitive modules are, with their specific domains, informational autarchy, and well-defined functions of generating basic representations, where the functions are carried out by specialized brain sites with a structural genetic basis. This is why, I suggested, cognitive modules are (or should be) intelligible *both* to classical cognitive science and the standard conception of evolution, which (I noted earlier in section 1.3) joins Darwin's theory of natural selection and structural genetics (Bogdan 1994, chapters 9 and 10).

Not accidentally, I think, we find a revealing counterpart convergence when it comes to the higher-level, nonmodular faculties of the intellect, such as Imagining. These faculties are in the business not of producing basic representations but rather of utilizing representations in further mentation and action. As Fodor (1983) argued, (classical) cognitive science does not know how to think of and theorize about intellectual faculties ("central systems," as he calls these faculties) because they have properties (most notably holistic interactivity, domain versatility, and informational promiscuity) that are not intelligible to (classical) cognitive science. And as the present book argued, the standard conception of evolution cannot plausibly explain the emergence of intellectual faculties, either.

The way out of this joint impasse, I argued in earlier chapters and other works, is a new evolutionary stance on ontogeny as developmental evolution: the devo-evo stance. Unlike the convergence between cognitive modularity and the action of natural selection, which may seem to make an evolutionary analysis almost redundant and dispensable, I think that the devo-evo stance on the ontogenetic construction of the intellect is indispensable. For only such a stance, scanning the strong pressures at work during distinct stages of human childhood—and in particular the sociocultural and sociopolitical pressures, which are the strongest—is likely to reveal ontogenetic solutions, if not adaptations, in the form of schemes for metamental rehearsals that become the initial matrices and incubators of later-developing intellectual faculties. I find the devo-evo stance indispensable for explaining other unique and exclusive outcomes of modern human ontogeny, such as language acquisition, predicative thinking, intuitive psychology, introspective thinking, and consciousness (Bogdan 1997, 2000, 2009, 2010).

From a wider evolutionary perspective, not necessarily tied to ontogeny, recent work has unearthed (what I would regard as) a variety of evolved initial matrices underlying a variety of intellectual or almost-intellectual faculties. These initial matrices turn out again to reflect more basic abilities that people are uniformly good at deploying and hence mental adaptations that respond to identifiable evolutionary pressures—not surprisingly, of a social nature in most cases. Among the most notable examples are cheating detection and other social contract algorithms underlying deontic and conditional reasoning (Cosmides 1989; Cummins 1996) as well as the evaluation of arguments in communication underlying the general ability to reason (Mercier and Sperber 2011). As in the case of strategizing versus Imagining, this research shows that people handle the precursor tasks typical of the initial matrices uniformly better than the successor tasks of the intellectual faculties built on their shoulders. I think that only an evolutionary analysis can spot this distinction and explain its rationale.

To sum up, it appears clearer than before, and certainly more apparent than during the first decades of classical cognitive science, that it takes an evolutionary archaeology of the human mind to begin to uncover as well as understand where intellectual faculties originate, in what shape and design, and why. But the importance of evolution is manifest not only in research and theorizing. It also matters to pedagogy. My classroom experience suggests that teaching cognitive science in evolutionary terms is much more fun, and much more of a mind opener and more integrative theoretically, for all those involved than teaching it in simplified, dry, slightly artificial, and sanitized classical terms. Evolutionary cognitive science is coming of age, and it is time for it to move into the mainstream of both research and pedagogy.

Appendix: Intuitive Psychology as Mind Designer

Directly and massively involved in the ontogenetic construction of mindvaulting, intuitive psychology is central to the argument of this book. Its contribution to mindvaulting is just one of several of its accomplishments as mind designer. Yet this role of mind designer is not widely noticed nor properly understood. One reason may be the fact that intuitive psychology is subject to divergent and often conflicting accounts, most of which fail to register its mind-design role. I see a basic and natural connection between the function and formats of intuitive psychology (for there are several), on the one hand, and its mind-design role, on the other hand. I also see a connection between distinct stages of development of intuitive psychology in childhood, with different formats of operation, and the distinct mental competencies it manages to design or help bring about during those stages. I will briefly outline these connections in what follows, and in the process, amplify and further clarify the account of intuitive psychology outlined in earlier chapters.

Before doing that, though, a reminder and a caveat. The reminder is about the central and consequential role of intuitive psychology in the mental life of children. This role, which makes the impact of intuitive psychology on mental development plausible and likely, reflects three key facts: that sociocultural and sociopolitical adaptation is most pressing and urgent for young human minds; that these minds cannot play and win this adaptation game without access and reaction to minds, both adult and young; and that such access and reaction to other minds, and later one's own, necessarily draw on interpreting mental states. Intuitive psychology is the competence evolved to register, interpret, and react to mental states.

The caveat concerns the angle on intuitive psychology taken in earlier chapters and below. It is mostly a *cognitive* angle insofar as it focuses on the recognition and interpretation of thoughts and attitudes as mental states related to concrete or abstract (propositional) targets. This angle is dictated by the hypothesis that it is this cognitive component of intuitive psychology that is essentially involved in its specific design of mindvaulting, itself a cognitive enterprise. Yet intuitive psychology is more than cognitive insofar as it also interprets emotions, moods, affects, and personality traits, and actually and often uses such noncognitive interpretations in its approach to thoughts and attitudes. But that is another story.

A.1   A Basic and Natural Connection

As I see the matter, there is a basic and natural connection between the overall job of intuitive psychology and its role of mind designer. The overall job is to adaptively and efficiently handle interpersonal relations, joint actions, imitation, education, the assimilation of culture, sociopolitics (as defined in earlier chapters), and in general whatever requires taking account of the mental states of others along with one's own in one's goal strategies and what one does. Modern humans are essentially social, political, and cultural animals, and they cannot instantiate these essential properties without being intuitive psychologists. Furthermore, and crucially, they cannot develop these essential properties in childhood without an avenue to other minds and later their own, which makes intuitive psychology an indispensable tool of mental development.

To discharge its sociocultural and political job, and integrate it in one's own goal strategies and actions in the relevant domains, intuitive psychology must be an eminently *practical* enterprise. This means that intuitive psychology evolved not only to interpret mental states, both of others and one's own, passively but also actively employ such interpretations as tool-like means to one's ends (Bogdan 1997, 2000, 2010). This practical role of guiding action in the social, political, and cultural domains has been widely ignored—or at best minimally and superficially acknowledged—in the philosophical and psychological literature, where most popular accounts are basically spectatorial; for them, the job of intuitive psychology is simply to register and represent, or simulate as well as explain and predict, mental states—full stop.

This does not make evolutionary sense. A major cognitive competence, such as intuitive psychology, has a selectable functional uptake in terms of its outputs and their impact on action. Natural and other forms of selection would not settle for less. Perception is for action to such an essential extent that it shares a common code with action. Registering someone's emotion frequently resonates in the observer's own similar emotion, and so on. Implemented by recently discovered mirroring mechanisms, such common coding and resonance abilities reflect as well as respond to evolutionary pressures to align inputs to outputs and representations to actions tightly and reliably (Prinz 2012). The same pressures act on intuitive psychology, particularly during ontogeny.

The functional uptake of intuitive psychology is to activate and guide goal strategies along with the resulting actions that involve people as well as their minds and actions, or more generally the goal strategies and actions that can be carried out only by reference to mental states. This means that the functional uptake is a key component of the cognitive schemes that implement intuitive-psychological interpretations of mental states. And being a key component means in turn that to be effective, the categories and schemes that interpret mental states must fit and service their functional uptake.

The implication that matters here is that the functional uptake is bound to shape the ways in which mental states are interpreted in appropriate categories and schemes, which is the *format* of interpretation of mental states. This is to say that people interpret mental states in terms in which and to the degree to which people can (in principle) do something about those mental states—act on, react to, think about, predict consequences, and so on—in ways that promote or guide their goal strategies. This aspect explains the practical or action-guiding format of intuitive-psychological categories and schemes. This format in turn begins to explain the mind-designing capability of intuitive psychology. As I see it, this capability develops along two routes.

The first route is *internal* to intuitive psychology, in that it takes off from inside its functional uptake. During childhood, when intuitive psychology takes shape, "doing something about mental states" and the goal strategies that draw on that "doing" graduate from simple to increasingly more complex, requiring a growing number of interactions with other mental abilities, such as language, memory, imagery, and reasoning. Under persistent ontogenetic pressures and set maturational patterns, some of these interacting abilities are recruited and orchestrated in durable mental schemes *within* the functional uptake of intuitive psychology, thus becoming potential templates and incubators for new mental competencies. I think that this is roughly how the mental scheme for word acquisition develops in early childhood out of the naive-psychological competence for shared attention and especially its attention-directing operation (Bogdan 2009), and also how reflexive thinking or thinking about one's thoughts develops later in childhood out of the commonsense-psychological ability for self-directed metarepresentation (Bogdan 2000).

Along the second *external* route, intuitive psychology is a major contributor. As their goal strategies in the sociocultural and political domains become more complicated, diversified, and demanding, children's minds recruit and orchestrate a diverse array of mental competencies into new forms and strategies of mentation, in which intuitive psychology is a major player. Consider strategizing as a telling example still fresh in the reader's mind. To do its work adaptively, in response to sociopolitical challenges, strategizing integrates several abilities, including the commonsense psychology of older children. The latter enables projections of mental states from inside the perspective of other mental states (the double-projection gambit of metamental rehearsals), which in turn becomes the hallmark of Imagination, once the resources for strategizing diversify and engage new domains. Assuming (at least for comparative purposes) that the much simpler relational thinking of chimpanzees (which one is friend/enemy with others, which one can be an ally in a fight, etc.) is a rudimentary form of strategizing (Byrne and Whiten 1988; Tomasello 1999), we can see how the injection of intuitive psychology (absent in apes) into such precursor thinking leads to a totally new form of strategizing and eventually Imagination, at least according to the argument of this book.

Along different lines, various mind-design contributions of intuitive psychology have been discussed by other researchers, such as Peter Hobson (1993), Katherine Nelson (1996, 2007), David Olson (1989), Josef Perner (1991, 2000), Wolfgang Prinz (2012), and Michael Tomasello (1999, 2003).

A.2 The Developmental Connection

The developmental fine-tuning of the mind-designing role of intuitive psychology necessarily depends on not only how and why this competence works but also *when* its constitutive abilities become operative and in *what format*. On both counts, the literature is rife with disagreements. I have tried in this book (and others) not to hold the mind-design analysis hostage—not too much anyway—to these disagreements and even conflicting readings of the evidence.

As an exercise in theoretical coherence, I have opted instead to rely more on a larger-picture view, in which what intuitive psychology does during a given age period and how it does it are measured against its most pressing challenges as well as a panoply of other competencies with which it intimately interacts or on which it depends. It is in this spirit that I want to motivate some distinctions made in earlier chapters along with some conjectures about the work and developmental timing of mindvaulting relative to the work and developmental timing of intuitive psychology as a designer of mindvaulting.

The trilateral view

The most popular accounts of intuitive psychology—the theory-theory view, simulation view, and modularity view—are *unitarian* in spirit, in the sense that they assume (but not quite prove) the *same* basic competence maturing organically throughout childhood and operating in adulthood. This does not make much developmental sense. In different age periods children are confronted with different social or interpersonal, cultural, and political challenges, and possess different mental resources to respond to these challenges. Intuitive psychology is no exception, in both how it operates and its interaction with other enabling abilities (language, memory, imagery, etc.) that it draws on to do its job. What unity there is to intuitive psychology has to do with its essential and permanent function—interpret mental states and factor them into one's goal strategies—and most likely its propensity to absorb and integrate earlier acquisitions into later developments.

The same is true of other mental competencies, such as language use and memory. Young children master phonetic, vocabulary, grammar, and a basic semantics in early years, and graduate to narratives and pragmatic discourse only later, yet narratives and pragmatic discourse are not organic maturations out of the early acquisitions; language use is not a unitarian affair. Likewise, children's early memory is semantic and episodic, and only later becomes autobiographical, but the latter is not an organic maturation of the former. Human memory is not a unitarian affair. Yet in both language use and memory, later acquisitions absorb and integrate earlier ones.

In a nonunitarian spirit, in section 2.4 I introduced a trilateral parsing of intuitive psychology into three successive capacities developing in three successive stages: a bilateral sense of mental states in early infancy (the first few months of life), the naive psychology of early childhood (from the first few months until around the age of four), and then a metarepresentational commonsense psychology (after four). This trilateral reading is admittedly based on a specific and not universally shared reading of the evidence. Although distinct in what they accomplish and how, the three competencies involved register and track as well as react to mental states. It is this shared function that in my view, renders them versions of intuitive psychology. And it is the shared function that most likely recruits and blends the abilities of the precursor version into the work of the successor one.

The *bilateral sense of mental states* does not track the world relatedness or world aboutness of those states but rather the interpersonal or I-You interactions. *Naive psychology* tracks both world relatedness and interpersonal relatedness, and does so in terms of overtly, usually visibly manifested relations of the mental states of (only) others to concrete, spatiotemporally defined targets (things, events, and situations). It is a situated expertise that is anchored primarily in the perceptuo-motor here and now (Perner 1991), and operates mostly procedurally, as a form of know-how, under rules that map stimuli onto appropriate recognitional categories—mostly of seeing, attention, simple desires, and visually based beliefs—and behavioral reactions (Bogdan 1997). Elsewhere I construed naive psychology as merely *metaintentional* or *metarelational* (but not metarepresentational) because it captures only the fact that another mind relates to a concrete target (object, event, or situation), but is unable to figure out how that mind represents the target from its perspective (Bogdan 2000, 105–114; 2003; 2010, 36–41).

In contrast, *commonsense psychology* registers, interprets, and reacts to complex, not necessarily visible attitudes (such as intentions, opinions, complex emotions, and the like) to targets that are not necessarily concrete, and does so mostly inferentially and metarepresentationally by taking the perspective of the thoughts as well as attitudes it envisages. It treats the thoughts and attitudes of others and selves in the same terms, with the same concepts.

As noted in section 6.3, I do not think that passing the visually based false-belief test between age three and four or earlier, even as early as twelve or eighteen months, indicates a competence for metarepresentation and the onset of (what I call) commonsense psychology. Remarkable as it is, passing the false-belief test is likely within the powers of a naive psychology by recruiting such resources as a grasp of another person's visual access (or lack of it), a sense that another person remembers what she saw, and a prediction that her visual memory will trigger an appropriate action (Bogdan 2003, 2010). These resources may even be present separately in the social cognition of apes, in which case, if apes consistently fail to pass the false-belief test (as it seems so far), it may be because, plausibly, they are not under strong enough pressures to assemble and routinize these resources, and systematically exploit their output.

In any event, it is not the false-belief test that (I think) best and earliest characterizes the uniqueness of human intuitive psychology but rather its starting platform: the bilateral sense of mental states.

A bilateral sense of mental states

My conjecture about infants' bilateral sense of mental states is mostly based on the remarkable and finely detailed work of Colwyn Trevarthen (1993, 2011) and Andrew Meltzoff and his collaborators (Meltzoff and Moore 1977; Meltzoff and Gopnik 1993). It is also based on my guess that this is when human infants begin implicitly to register and react to some mental invariants (initially intents, affects, and emotions) behind various communicative and behavioral manifestations, such as the same emotion variously displayed by eyes, face, smile, and gesture (Bogdan 2009). After a few months, infants become naive psychologists (in my terminology), and can recognize and follow gaze, register visual access or its absence, and detect simple desires. As social cognizers, chimpanzees also seem able to do most, if not all, of this (Tomasello and Call 1997), but for all we know to date, they don't appear to factor in the *mental* invariants into their recognition of gaze, visual access, or desire, and thus do not graduate to a naive *psych*ology. How do we know that? We conjecture in light of the implications of the apes' failure to factor a sense of the mental in an otherwise sophisticated social cognition, compared with the ability of young humans to do precisely that.

After all, what is recognition of attention basically but recognition of gaze plus mental intent, focus, and interest? Chimpanzees detect gaze but apparently not attention, and surely do not graduate to shared attention (Tomasello 1999); human children do both. Where is this critical difference coming from, since (to repeat) in the first two years or so, children's naive psychology is widely thought to cover largely the same territory of conspecific-world relations (gaze, visual access, simple desire, emotions, etc.) as chimpanzees do with their social cognition? I think that the bilateral sense of mental states is as good and plausible a conjecture about what makes the difference as any I have seen in the literature. This conjecture begins to explain why human naive psychology departs radically from its ape precursor and in turn starts to design a different sort of mind.

Others before self

The infantile sense of mental states concerns only others and so does the later developing naive psychology. In several works, I argued that these two early competencies are exclusively oriented toward the *other* (Bogdan 1997, 2000, 2005b, 2007, 2009, 2010). This is how I read the standard evidence surveyed in substantive and comprehensive works (Astington, Harris, and Olson 1988; Bjorklund 2005; Doherty 2009; Nelson 1996; Perner 1991; Tomasello 1999; Wellman 1990). From the larger-picture angle, I find that this external orientation makes devo-evo sense, since it is others (not selves) who both generate the strongest pressures and help manage them. From the same perspective, a close look at the basic coordinates of young cognition—such as online, largely stimulus-driven operation, anchored in current perception and motivation—also suggests an external orientation along with the lack of resources and indeed reasons for an introvert or self-directed cognition. The work of John Flavell and his team has also shown the lack of introspection and a poor sense of one's own thoughts before the five-to-six interval (Flavell et al. 1995). My own reading of the development of self-consciousness also points to the lack of an introvert self-consciousness before the age of four (Bogdan 2010).

A further but more controversial argument in the same direction concerns children's ability to self-ascribe attitudes metarepresentationally. I find both metarepresentation in general and self-ascriptions of attitudes in particular possible as well as effective only after the four-to-five interval. The consensus, at least in the so-called theory-theory and simulation corners, is that around three to four and possibly even earlier, children ascribe attitudes to others and themselves at the same time, with the same resources. In earlier works (Bogdan 2005b, 2007, 2010, chapter 3), I argued at length against this symmetry of dating and resources. In particular, I tried to show that famous experiments (such as the so-called Smarties experiment) meant to prove that around age four, if not earlier, children recognize their own false beliefs (and other attitudes), as they recognize those of others, actually measure only children's recognition and recall of their own prior *experiences* associated with past beliefs, and not the recognition of the *target relatedness* (or intentionality) of their past beliefs. The latter recognition, and hence the genuine understanding of one's own false belief (and other attitudes) emerges later than the recognition of the false beliefs (and other attitudes) of others. As far as I can tell, this distinction has been largely unnoticed in the literature and undermines the symmetry in question. Indeed, the sooner children recognize the false beliefs of others (with the simpler resources of naive psychology, as noted earlier), the more obvious becomes the gap in age and resources between that early recognition and the later recognition of their own false beliefs.

As argued earlier in chapter 6, under the label *change of mind*, it is a suite of radically new abilities, executive as well as cognitive, that make possible and effective children's turn toward their own minds, thoughts, and attitudes. This is to say that self-ascriptions of thoughts and attitudes (vital to Imagining) depend on developments not only in intuitive psychology but also in a suite of other enabling abilities.

A.3 Implications for Mindvaulting

I think that the tripartite segmentation of intuitive psychology just reviewed makes developmental sense and fits the earlier analysis of mindvaulting. Infants don't do mindvaulting and in particular pretending. One primary reason is that a bilateral sense of mind would not help with pretending and a naive psychology conducive to imitation is not yet in place. And when the latter is firmly in place during the second year, pretend play does indeed take off, and shares with naive psychology the same dominant and procedural perceptuomotor engagement with concrete objects and events. Young playful pretending is not Imaginative partly but essentially because its naive-psychological component is directed at other people's mental states, particularly in observation and imitation, and partly but equally essentially because the metarepresentational awareness of young children's own thoughts and attitudes, and the abilities to manipulate them in a tool-like manner in metamental rehearsals (abilities such as capacious working memory, introspection and deliberate, and reflective planning), are not yet operative.

Imagination itself was shown to abandon the concreteness of earlier situated and perceptuomotor engagements with concrete objects and events, to operate in a variety of domains and take the perspective of what is Imagined (among other novelties), only when a metarepresentational commonsense psychology emerges after the age of four. Even then, Imagination was conjectured to develop in two stages: first in an extrovert or outward-oriented mode, and later also in an introvert or inner-oriented mode, precisely because the commonsense psychology of older children transits from metarepresenting the mental states of others to metarepresenting one's own.

To sum up its mind-design role, in its different versions, at different ages, with different contributions, intuitive psychology seems to hold the key to the unique ontogenesis of a unique human mind. Mindvaulting is just one but very impressive and consequential outcome of this mind-design contribution.

Glossary

The glossary offers brief reminders of key notions, frequently employed and defined in terms specific to this inquiry, and indicates in square brackets in which chapter and section they were first introduced.

cause–causation actions
Actions intended to *cause* some external means, which are independent of one's body and its innate action schemes, to *cause* a desired end; tools are construed here as means used (only) in cause–causation actions [2.2]

Evolution (standard and new approaches)
The standard conception   Joins Darwin's theory of natural selection and structural genetics, and views natural selection as operating on variable traits that express structural genes, and in the mental domain end up installing specialized mechanisms such as "mental organs" or modules [1.3]

Evo-devo   The development of phenotypes depends on the turning on and off of structural genes by regulatory genes at different times and sites during development [1.4]

Eco-devo   Information in the genome is *functionally* intertwined with ecological influences at different stages of development, *in the sense that* reliable and recurrent features of external stimulation and experience at a stage constitute a sort of "ontogenetic niche" that is inherited together with the genome [1.4]

Devo-evo Tracks mental development along a sequence of ontogenetic niches, each with its own selection pressures, to which young minds develop responses as ontogenetic solutions, if not adaptations [1.4]

Foundations
Earlier and more basic mental abilities that evolved for their own reasons, having separately dedicated functions that are independent of their joint contribution to the metamental rehearsals that shape pretending and Imagining [chapters 4 and 6]

Imagination [always with a capital *I*]
The capacity to project offline thoughts about nonactual, possible, future, or counterfactual scenarios, and from their perspective and in their terms, further deploy such thoughts as tool-like means to ends in a deliberate, self-conscious, effortful, reflective, suppositional, and introspectively active form (also called productive, constructive, reflective, re-creative, or suppositional) [1.1]

imagination [with a small *i*]
Either the various outputs of the competence for Imagination, in the form of mental images, reenacted experiences, and fantasies, or else passive and unbidden mental projections, in the form of hallucinations, images, and dreams of day and night [3.1]

Imitation
Unlike the simpler mimicking and emulation learning, both limited to observable behaviors and their environmental effects, imitation also requires understanding the intended means–ends directedness of the object-manipulating behavior and thus presupposes an intuitive psychology [4.4]

Intellect
The set of high-level mental faculties involved in reasoning, deliberate planning, thoughtful communication, reflective problem solving and decision making, art creation, technological innovation, and scientific theorizing; Imagination is its engine [introduction]

Intuitive psychology (aka theory of mind or mindreading)
The ability to recognize and represent relations between minds, as in empathic communication, relations between another mind and the world, as in finding that somebody believes something, and relations among two or more minds and the world, as in shared attention; it comes in three versions: a bilateral sense of mental states in early infancy, naive psychology, until around the age of four, and commonsense psychology afterward [4.3]

Metamental rehearsal
Mental rehearsals consist in anticipating or projecting and inferring what could or will be done through some action, in some interaction with others, or in relating to an impending, future, or possible action or situation; metamental rehearsals are mental rehearsals that project thoughts that in turn project, in the sense that are about or factor in other thoughts and mental states, which is why they are said to operate by double projection [3.3]

Metarepresentation
Construed here as the intuitive-psychological ability to represent some mental state (thought, attitude, or emotion) in its relation to some target (fact, event, or situation), from its perspective and terms; it begins with the mental states of others in midchildhood and later applies to one's own mental states; it is part of commonsense but not early naive psychology [6.3 and 6.4]

Projection
The brain's intrinsic propensity, constantly exercised, to anticipate and predict actions, experiences, and states of the environment along with their impact on the organism [4.1]

Strategizing
Mentally figuring out and rehearsing how to handle the thoughts, attitudes, utterances, and actions of others, and in response, those of one's own; strategizing is metamentally rehearsing offline how to reach one's goals by means of others, and also how to enable or influence others to reach their goals by means of oneself, either altruistically, cooperatively, or with ulterior selfish motives [7.3]

Suppositional stance
Deliberately, introspectively, and explicitly opening a separate mental file in which to represent some possible or future state of affairs, with a full metarepresentational sense of what one is doing (see *metarepresentation*), while at the same time managing one's current and real-world-bound perception, thinking, and behavior; based on the ontogeny of metarepresentation, the suppositional stance develops only after age four, being first world bound or extrovert, and later also mind bound or introvert [5.2, 6.3, and 6.4]

References

Adamson, L. B. 1995. *Communication Development during Infancy*. Boulder, CO: Westview Press.

Addis, D. R., A. T. Wong, and D. L. S. Schacter. 2007. Remembering the Past and Imagining the Future. *Neuropsychologia* 45:1363–1377.

Anderson, M. 2010. Neural Reuse: A Fundamental Organizational Principle of the Brain. *Behavioral and Brain Sciences* 33:245–266.

Astington, J., and A. Gopnik. 1988. Knowing You've Changed Your Mind. In *Developing Theories of Mind*, ed. J. Astington et al. Cambridge: Cambridge University Press.

Astington, J., P. Harris, and D. Olson. 1988. *Developing Theories of Mind*. Cambridge: Cambridge University Press.

Atance, C. M. 2008. From Past into the Future: the Developmental Origins and Trajectory of Future Episodic Thinking. In *Handbook of Episodic Memory*, ed. E. Dere et al., vol. 18. Dordrecht: Elsevier.

Atance, C. M., and L. K. Jackson. 2009. The Development and Coherence of Future-Oriented Behaviors in Preschool Years. *Journal of Experimental Child Psychology* 102:379–391.

Atance, C. M., and A. N. Meltzoff. 2006. Preschoolers' Current Desires Warp Their Choices for the Future. *Psychological Science* 17:583–587.

Baillargeon, R., R. M. Scott, and Z. He. 2010. False-Belief Understanding in Infants. *Trends in Cognitive Sciences* 14:110–118.

Baird, B., J. Smallwood, and J. W. Schooler. 2011. Back to the Future: Autobiographical Planning and the Functionality of Mind-Wandering. *Consciousness and Cognition* 20:1604–1611.

Bar, M. 2007. The Proactive Brain. *Trends in Cognitive Sciences* 11:280–289.

Bar, M. 2009. The Proactive Brain: Memory for Predictions. *Philosophical Transactions of the Royal Society* 364:1235–1243.

Bar, M., ed. 2011. *Predictions in the Brain*. Oxford: Oxford University Press.

Baron-Cohen, S. 1995. *Mindblindness*. Cambridge, MA: MIT Press.

Bates, E. 1976. *Language and Context*. New York: Academic Press.

Beck, S. R., E. J. Robinson, D. J. Carroll, and I. A. Apperly. 2006. Children's Thinking about Counterfactuals and Future Hypotheticals as Possibilities. *Child Development* 77:413–426.

Bermúdez, J. 2003. *Thoughts without Words*. Oxford: Oxford University Press.

Bjorklund, D. F. 2005. *Children's Thinking*. Pacific Grove, CA: Brooks/Cole.

Bjorklund, D. F., and A. Pellegrini. 2001. *The Origins of Human Nature*. Washington, DC: American Psychological Association.

Bogdan, R. J. 1994. *Grounds for Cognition*. Hillsdale, NJ: Erlbaum.

Bogdan, R. J. 1997. *Interpreting Minds*. Cambridge, MA: MIT Press.

Bogdan, R. J. 2000. *Minding Minds*. Cambridge, MA: MIT Press.

Bogdan, R. J. 2001. Developing Mental Abilities by Representing Intentionality. *Synthese* 129:233–258.

Bogdan, R. J. 2003. Watch Your Metastep: The First-Order Limits of Early Intentional Attributions. In *Persons*, ed. C. Kanzian et al. Vienna: Holder-Pichler-Tempsky.

Bogdan, R. J. 2005a. Pretending as Imaginative Rehearsal for Cultural Conformity. *Journal of Cognition and Culture* 5:191–213.

Bogdan, R. J. 2005b. Why Self-ascriptions Are Difficult and Develop Late. In *Other Minds*, ed. B. Malle and S. Hodges. New York: Guilford Press.

Bogdan, R. J. 2007. Inside Loops. *Synthese* 159:235–252.

Bogdan, R. J. 2009. *Predicative Minds*. Cambridge, MA: MIT Press.

Bogdan, R. J. 2010. *Our Own Minds*. Cambridge, MA: MIT Press.

Bogdan, R. J. 2012. Self-consciousness: Executive Design, Sociocultural Grounds (and Responses to Commentators). http://consciousnessonline.com/2012/02/17/self-consciousness-executive-design-socioculturalgrounds/.

Bornstein, M. H. 2006. On the Significance of Social Relationhips in the Development of Children's Earliest Symbolic Play. In *Play and Development*, ed. A. Göncü and S. Gaskinds. Mahwah, NJ: Erlbaum.

Boyd, R., and J. B. Silk. 1997. *How Humans Evolved*. New York: Norton.

Brann, E.T.H. 1991. *The World of the Imagination*. Lanham, MD: Rowman and Littlefield.

Bruner, J. 1983. *Child's Talk*. New York: Norton.

Bruner, J. 1990. *Acts of Meaning*. Cambridge, MA: Harvard University Press.

Bruner, J., and C. Feldman. 1993. Theories of Mind and the Problems of Autism. In *Understanding Other Minds*, ed. S. Baron-Cohen et al. Oxford: Oxford University Press.

Buckner, R. L., and D. C. Carroll. 2007. Self-projection and the Brain. *Trends in Cognitive Sciences* 11:49–56.

Byrne, R., and A. Whiten, eds. 1988. *Machiavellian Intelligence*. Oxford: Oxford University Press.

Byrne, R., and A. Whiten. 1991. Computation and Mindreading in Primate Tactical Deception. In *Natural Theories of Mind*, ed. A. Whiten. Oxford: Blackwell.

Carey, S. 2009. *The Origin of Concepts*. Oxford: Oxford University Press.

Carpenter, M., N. Akhtar, and M. Tomasello. 1998. Fourteen-through-Eighteen-Month-Old Infants Differentially Imitate Intentional and Accidental Actions. *Infant Behavior and Development* 21:315–330.

Carroll, S. 2005. *Endless Forms Most Beautiful*. New York: Norton.

Carruthers, P. 1996. *Language, Thought, and Consciousness*. Cambridge: Cambridge University Press.

Carruthers, P. 2002. Human Creativity: Its Cognitive Basis, Its Evolution, and Its Connections with Childhood Pretence. *British Journal for the Philosophy of Science* 53:225–249.

Carruthers, P. 2005. *Consciousness: Essays from a Higher-Order Perspective*. Oxford: Oxford University Press.

Casey, E. 1973. *Imagining*. Bloomington: Indiana University Press.

Changeux, J.-P. 1985. *The Neuronal Man*. Oxford: Oxford University Press.

Cheney, D., and R. Seyfarth. 1990. *How Monkeys See the World*. Chicago: University of Chicago Press.

Chomsky, N. 1988. *Language and Problems of Knowledge*. Cambridge, MA: MIT Press.

Conway, M. 2002. Sensory-perceptual Memory and Its Context: Autobiographical Memory. In *Episodic Memory*, ed. A. Baddeley et al. Oxford: Oxford University Press.

Coolidge, F., and T. Wynn. 2009. *The Rise of Homo Sapiens*. London: Wiley-Blackwell.

Cosmides, L. 1989. The Logic of Social Exchange. *Cognition* 31:187–276.

Cosmides, L., and J. Tooby. 2000. Consider the Source: The Evolution of Adaptations for Decoupling and Metarepresentations. In *Metarepresentations*, ed. D. Sperber. Oxford: Oxford University Press.

Cummins, D. 1996. Evidence for the Innateness of Deontic Reasoning. *Mind and Language* 11:160–190.

Currie, G., and I. Ravenscroft. 2002. *Recreative Minds*. Oxford: Oxford University Press.

Dehaene, S. 1997/2011. *The Number Sense*. Oxford: Oxford University Press.

DeLoache, J. S. 1995. Early Understanding and Use of Symbols. *Current Directions in Psychological Science* 4:109–113.

Dennett, D. 1991. *Consciousness Explained*. Boston: Little, Brown.

de Vignemont, F., and P. Fourneret. 2004. The Sense of Agency. *Consciousness and Cognition* 13:1–19.

Diamond, A. 2001. Normal Developments of Prefrontal Cortex from Birth to Young Adulthood. In *The Frontal Lobes*, ed. D. T. Stuss and R. T. Knight. Oxford: Oxford University Press.

Doherty, M. J. 2009. *Theory of Mind*. Hove, UK: Psychology Press.

Donald, M. 2001. *A Mind So Rare*. New York: Norton.

Engel, S. 2005. The Narrative Worlds of *What Is* and *What If*. *Cognitive Development* 20:514–525.

Fivush, R. 2011. The Development of Autobiographical Memory. *Annual Review of Psychology* 62:559–582.

Flavell, J. H., F. L. Green, and E. R. Flavell. 1995. *Young Children's Knowledge about Thinking*. Chicago: University of Chicago Press.

Fodor, J. 1983. *The Modularity of Mind*. Cambridge, MA: MIT Press.

Ganis, G., et al. 2003. Neural Correlates of Different Types of Deception. *Cerebral Cortex* 13:830–836.

Goldberg, E. 2001. *The Executive Brain: Frontal Lobes and the Civilized Mind.* Oxford: Oxford University Press.

Goldman, A. 1993. The Psychology of Folk Psychology. *Behavioral and Brain Sciences* 16:15–28.

Goldman, A. 2006. *Simulating Minds.* Oxford: Oxford University Press.

Gomez, J. C. 2008. The Evolution of Pretence: From Intentional Availability to Intentional Non-existence. *Mind and Language* 23:586–606.

Gordon, R. M. 1986. Folk Psychology as Simulation. Mind and Language 1:158–171.

Grush, R. 2004. The Emulation Theory of Representation. *Behavioral and Brain Sciences* 27:377–442.

Harris, J. R. 1995. Where Is the Child's Environment? A Group Socialization Theory of Development. *Psychological Review* 102:458–489.

Harris, J. R. 1998. *The Nurture Assumption: Why Children Turn Out the Way They Do.* New York: Free Press.

Harris, P. 2000. *The Work of Imagination.* Oxford: Blackwell.

Harris, P. 2006. Hard Work for the Imagination. In *Play and Development,* ed. A. Göncü and S. Gaskinds. Mahwah, NJ: Erlbaum.

Hesslow, G. 2002. Conscious Thought as Simulation of Behavior and Perception. *Trends in Cognitive Sciences* 6:242–247.

Heyes, C. 1951. *The Ape in Our House.* New York: Harper and Brothers.

Hobson, R. P. 1993. *Autism and the Development of Mind.* Hillsdale, NJ: Erlbaum.

Hopkins, W. D., J. Fagot, and J. Vauclair. 1993. Mirror-Image Matching and Mental Rotation Problem Solving by Baboons. *Journal of Experimental Psychology: General* 122:61–72.

Jeannerod, M. 2006. *Motor Cognition*. Oxford: Oxford University Press.

Karmiloff-Smith, A. 1992. *Beyond Modularity*. Cambridge, MA: MIT Press.

Kavanaugh, R. D., and S. Engel. 1998. The Development of Pretense and Narrative in Early Childhood. In *Multiple Perspectives on Play in Early Childhood Education*, ed. O. N. Saracho and B. Spodek. Albany: State University of New York Press.

Klein, R. G., with B. Edgar. 2002. *The Dawn of Culture*. New York: Wiley.

Konner, M. 2010. *The Evolution of Childhood*. Cambridge, MA: Harvard University Press.

Lautrey, J., and D. Chartier. 1987. Images mentales de transformations et operations cognitives. *L'Année Psychologique* 87:581–602.

Leekam, S. 1991. Jokes and Lies: Children's Understanding of Intentional Falsehood. In *Natural Theories of Mind*, ed. A. Whiten. Oxford: Blackwell.

Leslie, A. M. 1988. Some Implications of Pretense for Mechanisms Underlying the Child's Theory of Mind. In *Developing Theories of Mind*, ed. J. W. Astington et al. Cambridge: Cambridge University Press.

Lickliter, R., and C. Harshaw. 2010. Canalization and Malleability Reconsidered. In *Handbook of Developmental Science, Behavior, and Genetics*, ed. K. E. Hood et al. Oxford: Blackwell.

Lillard, A. 1993. Young Children's Conceptualization of Pretence. *Child Development* 64:372–386.

Lillard, A. 1994. Making Sense of Pretense. In *Children's Early Understanding of Mind*, ed. C. Lewis and P. Mitchell. Hillsdale, NJ: Erlbaum.

Locke, J. L., and B. Bogin. 2006. Language and Life History. *Behavioral and Brain Sciences* 29:259–325.

Luna, B., et al. 2001. Maturation of Widely Distributed Brain Function Subserves Cognitive Development. *NeuroImage* 13 (5): 786–793.

Luria, A. R. 1934. The Second Psychological Expedition to Central Asia. *Journal of Genetic Psychology* 41:255–259.

Marcovitch, S., and D. J. Lewkowicz. 2004. U-Shaped Functions: Artifact or Hallmark of Development? *Journal of Cognition and Development* 5:113–118.

Maynard, D. W. 1985. On the Functions of Social Conflict among Children. *American Sociological Review* 50:207–223.

McGinn, C. 2004. *Mindsight*. Cambridge, MA: Harvard University Press.

Meltzoff, A. 1995. Understanding the Intentions of Others. *Developmental Psychology* 31:838–850.

Meltzoff, A., and A. Gopnik. 1993. The Role of Imitation in Understanding Persons and Developing a Theory of Mind. In *Understanding Other Minds*, ed. S. Baron-Cohen et al. Oxford: Oxford University Press.

Meltzoff, A., and M. Moore. 1977. Imitation of Facial and Manual Gestures by Human Neonates. *Science* 198:75–78.

Mercier, H. 2011. Reasoning Serves Argumentation in Children. *Cognitive Development* 26:177–191.

Mercier, H., and D. Sperber. 2011. Why Do Humans Reason? Arguments for an Argumentative Theory. *Behavioral and Brain Sciences* 34:57–111.

Michel, G. F. 2010. The Roles of Environment, Experience, and Learning in Behavioral Development. In *Handbook of Developmental Science, Behavior, and Genetics*, ed. K. E. Hood et al. Oxford: Blackwell.

Mitchell, R. W., ed. 2002. *Pretending and Imagination in Animals and Children*. Cambridge: Cambridge University Press.

Mitchell, R. W. 2006. Pretense in Animals. In *Play and Development*, ed. A. Göncü and S. Gaskinds. Mahwah, NJ: Erlbaum.

Mithen, S. 1996. *Prehistory of the Mind*. London: Thames.

Nelson, K. 1986. *Event Knowledge*. Hillsdale, NJ: Erlbaum.

Nelson, K. 1992. Emergence of Autobiographical Memory at Age Four. *Human Development* 35:172–177.

Nelson, K. 1996. *Language in Cognitive Development*. Cambridge: Cambridge University Press.

Nelson, K. 2007. *Young Minds in Social Worlds*. Cambridge, MA: Harvard University Press.

Nelson, K., and R. Fivush. 2004. The Emergence of Autobiographical Memory. *Psychological Review* 111:486–511.

Newcombe, N. S., and J. Huttenlocher. 2006. Development of Spatial Cognition. In Handbook of Child Psychology, ed. D. Kuhn and R. S. Siegler. New York: Wiley.

Nichols, S., ed. 2006. *The Architecture of the Imagination*. Oxford: Oxford University Press.

Nicolopoulou, A. 2006. The Interplay of Play and Narrative in Children's Development. In *Play and Development*, ed. A. Göncü and S. Gaskins. Mahwah, NJ: Erlbaum.

Olson, D. 1989. Making Up Your Mind. *Canadian Psychology* 30:617–627.

Oppenheim, R. W. 1981. Ontogenetic Adaptations and Retrogressive Processes in the Development of the Nervous System and Behavior. In *Maturation and Development*, ed. K. J. Connely and H. Prechtl. Philadelphia: International Medical.

Paley, V. G. 1990. *The Boy Who Would Be a Helicopter*. Cambridge, MA: Harvard University Press.

Perner, J. 1988. Higher-Order Beliefs and Intentions in Children's Understanding of Social Interactions. In *Developing Theories of Mind*, ed. J. Astington et al. Cambridge: Cambridge University Press.

Perner, J. 1991. *Understanding the Representational Mind*. Cambridge, MA: MIT Press.

Perner, J. 2000. Memory and Theory of Mind. In *The Oxford Handbook of Memory*, ed. E. Tulving et al. Oxford: Oxford University Press.

Peskin, J. 1992. Ruse and Representation: On Children's Ability to Conceal Information. *Developmental Psychology* 28:84–89.

Piaget, J. 1945/1962. *Play, Dreams, and Imitation*. London: Routledge and Kegan Paul.

Piaget, J. 1964. *Six Etudes de Psychologie*. Geneva: Editions Gonthier.

Piaget, J. 1974. *Understanding Causality*. New York: Norton.

Pinker, S., and P. Bloom. 1990. Natural Language and Natural Selection. *Behavioral and Brain Sciences* 13:707–784.

Piolino, P., et al. 2007. Do School-age Children Remember or Know the Personal Past? *Consciousness and Cognition* 16:84–101.

Polack, A., and P. Harris. 1999. Deception by Young Children following Noncompliance. *Developmental Psychology* 35:561–568.

Preuss, T., M. Caceres, M. Oldham, and D. Geschwind. 2004. Human Brain Evolution. *Nature Reviews: Genetics* 5:850–866.

Prinz, W. 2012. *Open Minds*. Cambridge, MA: MIT Press.

Raichle, M., and A. Snyder. 2007. A Default Mode of Brain Function. *NeuroImage* 37 (4): 1083–1090.

Riggs, K. J., and S. R. Beck. 2007. Thinking Developmentally about Counterfactual Possibilities. *Behavioral and Brain Sciences* 30:463–464.

Rogoff, B. 1990. *Apprenticeship in Thinking*. Oxford: Oxford University Press.

Sameroff, A. J., and M. M. Haith, eds. 1996. *The Five to Seven Year Shift*. Chicago: University of Chicago Press.

Savage-Rumbaugh, S., and R. Lewin. 1996. *Kanzi*. New York: Wiley.

Searle, J. 1983. *Intentionality*. Cambridge: Cambridge University Press.

Shettleworth, S. 2010. *Cognition, Evolution, and Behavior*. 2nd ed. New York: Oxford University Press.

Smith, P. K. 2010. *Children and Play*. Chichester, UK: Wiley-Blackwell.

Sodian, B., C. Taylor, P. Harris, and J. Perner. 1991. Early Deception and the Child's Theory of Mind. *Child Development* 62:468–483.

Sperry, R. W. 1950. Neural Basis of the Spontaneous Optokinetic Response Produced by Visual Inversion. *Journal of Comparative and Physiological Psychology* 43:482–489.

Suddendorf, T., and M. C. Corballis. 2007. The Evolution of Foresight: What Is Mental Time Travel, and Is It Unique to Humans? *Behavioral and Brain Sciences* 30:299–314.

Sullivan, K., and E. Winner. 1991. When Three-Year-Olds Understand Ignorance, False Belief, and Representational Change. *British Journal of Developmental Psychology* 9:159–171.

Taylor, M. 1999. *Imaginary Companions and the Children Who Create Them*. New York: Oxford University Press.

Taylor, M., S. M. Carlson, and A. B. Shawber. 2007. Autonomy and Control in Children's Interactions with Imaginary Companions. In *Imaginative Minds*, ed. I. Roth. New York: Oxford University Press.

Tomasello, M. 1999. *The Cultural Origins of Human Cognition*. Cambridge, MA: Harvard University Press.

Tomasello, M. 2003. *Constructing a Language*. Cambridge, MA: Harvard University Press.

Tomasello, M., and J. Call. 1997. *Primate Cognition*. New York: Oxford University Press.

Trevarthen, C. 1993. The Self Born in Intersubjectivity. In *The Perceived Self*, ed. U. Neisser. Cambridge: Cambridge University Press.

Trevarthen, C. 2011. The Generation of Human Meaning. In *Joint Attention*, ed. A. Seemann. Cambridge, MA: MIT Press.

Tulving, E. 2005. Episodic Memory and Autonoesis: Uniquely Human?
In *The Missing Link in Cognition: Origins of Self-reflective Consciousness*, ed.
H. S. Terrace and J. Metcalfe. Oxford: Oxford University Press.

von Holst, E., and H. Mittelstaedt. 1950. Das reafferenzprinzip: Wech-
selwirkungen zwischen zentralnervensystem und peripherie. *Naturwis-
senschaften* 37:464–476.

Vygotsky, L. 1935/1978. Interaction between Learning and Development. In *Mind in Society*. Cambridge, MA: Harvard University Press.

Wellman, H. 1990. *The Child's Theory of Mind*. Cambridge, MA: MIT
Press.

West, M. J., and A. P. King. 1987. Settling Nature and Nurture into an
Ontogenetic Niche. *Developmental Psychobiology* 20:549–562.

West-Eberhard, M. J. 2003. *Developmental Plasticity and Evolution*. New
York: Oxford University Press.

Whiten, A., ed. 1991. *Natural Theories of Mind*. Oxford: Blackwell.

Williams, J. M., et al. 1996. The Specificity of Autobiographical Memory
and Imageability of the Future. *Memory and Cognition* 24:116–125.

Zelazo, P. L., et al., eds. *Developing Theories of Intention*. Mahwah, NJ:
Erlbaum.

Zwaan, R. A. 1999. Situation Models: The Mental Leap into Imagined
Worlds. *Current Directions in Psychological Science* 8:15–18.

Index

Addis, D., 173
Anderson, M., 25, 26
Animal minds, 53–55
Apes, enculturation of, 30–34. *See also* Kanzi
Assembly, 22–27
  brain propensity for, 24–26
  of number sense, 23 *(see also* Dehaene, S.)
Autobiographical memory, 160–161, 170–175

Baird, B., 174
Bar, M., 62, 79, 173
Baron-Cohen, S., 121
Bjorklund, D., 22, 25, 148, 178
Bloom, P., 14
Bornstein, M., 85, 110
Bruner, J., 40, 186

Call, J., 30, 108, 114, 116
Carroll, S., 17
Carruthers, P., 102, 108, 112, 115, 137

Changeux, J-P., 26
Chomsky, N., 14
Coolidge, F., 14, 89
Cosmides, L., 102, 103, 201
Counterfactual thinking, 143
Cummins, D., 201
Currie, G., 124

Dehaene, S., 23, 26, 27
DeLoache, J., 111
Dennett, D., 14, 26
Descartes, R., 51
Developmental evolutionary theory (devo-evo), 20–21
Donald, M., 148

Ecological developmental biology (eco-devo), 18–19
Engel, S., 109, 131
Epigenetic markers, 18
Evolutionary developmental biology (evo-devo), 17–18
Executive abilities, 93–94, 145–149

Fivush, R., 171, 172, 174
Flavell, J., 89, 213
Fodor, J., 12, 199, 200
Freud, S., 51

Ganis, G., 175, 180
Genome
  regulatory, 17, 19–20
  structural, 12, 15, 19–20
Goldman, A., 52, 89

Harris, J., 164, 165, 180
Harris, P., 100, 102, 108, 109,
  110, 112, 129, 130, 152, 155,
  167, 186
Harshaw, C., 18
Heterochrony, 25
Hobson, P., 110, 121, 208

Imaginary companions,
  167–170
Imagination
  as competence, 56–58, 60–61
  competence transfer from
    strategizing, 187–194
  cognitive abilities of, 140
  enactive, 52
  executive abilities of, 139–140
  imagistic, 49–50
  introvert, 158–160
  noncognitive, 52
  vs. prediction, 53
  propositional (suppositional),
    50–51
Imitation, 90–92, 120
Intellect, 5

Intuitive psychology (a.k.a.
  theory of mind), 42–46
  basics of, 42–43
  as commonsense psychology,
    159
  vs. imaginative simulation,
    88–90
  as mind designer, 204–208, 215
  as naïve psychology, 87–90
  others-self asymmetry, 213–215
  three forms and stages of,
    44–46, 209–213

Jeannerod, M., 82, 83
Juvenile sociopolitics, 164–167

Kant, I., 49, 50
Kanzi, 31–34
Karmiloff-Smith, A., 143
King, A., 18
Klein, R., 14

Leekam, S., 181
Leslie, A., 102, 110–111, 152
Lewkowitz, D., 22
Lickliter, R., 18
Lillard, A., 102, 108, 111, 114
Luria, A., 155

Markovitch, S., 22
Maynard, D., 165, 180
Meltzoff, A., 44, 100, 128, 212
Mental imagery, 142
Mercier, H., 178, 201
Metamental rehearsals, 48, 62–64
  reasons for, 68–70

Metarepresentation
  of other minds, 149–152
  vs. suppositional stance,
    151–152 (*see also* Suppositional
    stance)
  tasks of, 153–158
Michel, G., 18
Mitchell, R., 108
Mittelstaedt, H., 80

Narration, 186–187
  script narrativity, 129–131
Nelson, K., 40, 114, 115, 129,
  172, 186, 208
Nicolopoulou, A., 129

Olson, D., 208
Ontogenetic adaptations, 21–22
Ontogenetic solutions, 21–22,
  24
Oppenheim, R., 21

Paley, V., 129
Pellegrini, A., 22, 25, 148
Perner, J., 86, 111, 124, 147, 160,
  172, 182, 208, 210
Peskin, J., 180
Piaget, J., 35–37, 40, 51, 64, 110,
  111
  on cause-causation actions, 37
  on mental activism, 36
Pinker, S., 14
Plato, 51
Play, 83–87
  exploratory, 101, 106, 113, 116,
    117, 122

Pretend play
  action angle on, 113–116
  contributions to Imagination,
    127–133
  different views about, 102–103,
    108
  intentional envelope of, 132
  limitations of, 124–126
  as role impersonation in
    sociocultural action, 117–122
  sociocultural grounds of,
    100–106
  tasks of, 122–123
Pretend stance, 101, 106, 117,
  118, 120–122, 152
  views about, 109–113
Preuss, T., 20
Prinz, W., 206, 208
Projection, 78–83
Puzzles about Imagination
  developmental, 13
  evolutionary, in general, 9–10
  genetic, 12
  historical, 11
  neuropsychological, 11–12

Ravenscroft, I., 124
Representational re-description,
  143–144

Searle, J., 82
Sperber, D., 201
Sperry, R., 80
Strategizing, 175–179
  lying, 179–182
  tasks of, 183–187

Sullivan, K., 180
Suppositional stance, 113, 125,
    150, 152, 153, 154, 157
  in illiterate people, 156

Taylor, M., 167, 169
Thoughts
  as mental tools, 40–41, 46,
    64–67
Tomasello, M., 30, 37, 65, 86,
    108, 110, 114, 115, 116, 132,
    192, 208, 212
  on imitation, 91–92, 107
Tooby, J., 102, 103
Trevarthen, C., 44, 100, 212

Von Holst, E., 80
Vygotsky, L., 52, 133–134, 155,
    156

West, M., 18, 25
Wynn, T., 14, 89

Zone of proximal development,
    133–135